Praise for *Sustainability Essentials*

"This is a great leadership guide for lawyers. The test for any lawyer is ethics, leadership, and sustainable development."

—Leon E. Panetta, Chairman, The Panetta Institute; Former U.S. Secretary of Defense

"The urgency to integrate sustainability into the forefront of business decision making has never been greater, and this book uniquely contributes to this goal."

—Roger Martella, Vice President and Chief Sustainability Officer, General Electric; Former General Counsel, EPA

"This is a must read for any attorney or legal professional who needs the easy, quick how-to on integrating sustainable development within legal practices."

—Gayatri Joshi, Executive Director of the Law Firm Sustainability Network; Vice President of Vorgate LLC

"This book provides an empowering blueprint for any lawyer seeking to integrate climate justice into every dimension of their work."

—Tim Hirschel-Burns, Amelia Keyes, and **Devin Oliver,** Law Students for Climate Accountability

"Many lawyers, regardless of their specialties or the stage of their careers, hunger to use their professional skills and develop new ones to address climate change and other environmental threats. Built on the pillars of sustainable development, ethics, and leadership, this deeply researched book provides pathways for lawyers to pursue this goal."

—Michael Gerrard, Columbia Law School Professor; Faculty Director, Sabin Center for Climate Change Law

"I am heartened to see a new generation of lawyers seeking to be effective in advancing sustainable development goals in their daily life work. In this book they will find both theory and practical ideas for making a difference."

—Mary D. Nichols, Former Chair, California Air Resources Board

"If law is the heart of the legal practice, then sustainability may well be its soul, moving lawyers toward a legacy of conscious commitment to vital and necessary change to transform society. This guide, by three of the most well-known sustainability, leadership, and ethical practitioners in the country, is a helpful walking stick on the pathway to sustainability."

—John C. Cruden, Former Assistant Attorney General, U.S. Department of Justice

"This book updates both the theory and practice of law so that it can embody a missing set of values—such as offering future generations a livable earth. It is not just timely; it is overdue."

—**Hal Harvey,** CEO, Energy Innovation

"We need a new generation of lawyers who recognize that we can create the power to confront the climate crisis, the governance crisis, and other existential threats only by combining sound lawyering with organization. This book is an important step in the right direction."

—**Marshall Ganz,** Senior Lecturer in Leadership, Organizing, and Civil Society, Harvard Kennedy School of Government

"Sustainable development has emerged as a foundational framework for life in the 21st century—and this Leadership Guide for Lawyers offers clear and comprehensive guidance to law students and attorneys in a wide range of settings about how to make sense of this multidimensional concept and fold its principles into their work and professional lives."

—**Daniel C. Esty,** Hillhouse Professor of Environmental Law and Policy at Yale University; Former Commissioner, Connecticut Department of Energy and Environmental Protection

"This guidebook is long overdue, thank you! It's high time more lawyers learn to organize and lead the systemic changes we need in the 21st century. This book shows the way!"

—**Kathleen Rogers,** President, Earth Day Network

"As law students, we're taught that law structures society. Hardly—if ever—are we taught how to use the law to restructure society in a sustainable way. This guide not only explains how the law can be used to restructure society more sustainably, but also posits that this is the ethical duty of every lawyer."

—**Minha Jutt** and **Chloe Ketchmark,**
University of Kansas School of Law, Class of 2022

"Lawyers and their clients talk a lot about sustainability, but what does that mean in practical terms? Dernbach, Bogoshian, and Russell answer that question and provide a real-world guide in this admirable volume."

—**Ken Alex,** Director, Project Climate at UC Berkeley; Former Senior Policy Advisor, California Governor Jerry Brown

"Hello to the curious and hopeful—this book is for you! It has all that you need to know on how to become a part of the movement that creates a more wonderful and sustainable planet for us all!"

—**Arlena Barnes,** Former Senior Attorney, Bonneville Power Administration

"Innovative, practical, and principled, *Sustainability Essentials* offers a blueprint for the ethical practice of law while promoting sustainable development."

—**Kevin R. Johnson,** Dean and Mabie-Apallas Professor of Public Interest Law and Chicana/o Studies, UC Davis School of Law

"More than a call to action, *Sustainability Essentials* gives law students, legal practitioners, and emerging leaders the essential, practical tools to apply this framework without losing sight of the urgency of making our world a better place."

—**Randall Winston,** Attorney, O'Melveny & Myers LLP; Advisory Board Member, Center for Law, Energy & the Environment at Berkeley Law

"For too long, many lawyers have forsaken the role of leadership in service of their client needs, trending instead towards reactive lawyering and counseling. This book presents the strong and cogent case for leadership, focusing on the meaningful roles lawyers can—and should—play in our quest for a sustainable future."

—**Avi Garbow,** President, Resources Legacy Fund; Former EPA General Counsel; Former Environmental Advocate at Patagonia

"Corporate leaders need their lawyers to read this practical book and apply it! Only with leadership can we accelerate our transition to a sustainable society."

—**Lenny Mendonca,** Former Chief Economic and Business Advisor, State of California

"This guide, *Sustainability Essentials*, is an invaluable resource for all of us working to build a better future."

—**Fred Kenney,** Director, Legal and External Affairs, International Maritime Organization; Former U.S. Coast Guard Admiral and Judge Advocate General

Sustainability ESSENTIALS

A Leadership Guide for Lawyers

John C. Dernbach, Matthew Bogoshian, and Irma Russell

AMERICAN BAR ASSOCIATION
Environment Energy and Resources Section

Cover design by Jill Tedhams/ABA Design

Printed in the United States of America.

26 25 24 23   5 4 3 2

Library of Congress Cataloging-in-Publication Data

Names: Dernbach, John C., 1953- author. | Bogoshian, Matthew, author. | Russell, Irma S., author. | American Bar Association Environment Energy and Resources Section, sponsoring body.
Title: Sustainability essentials : a leadership guide for lawyers / John C. Dernbach, Matthew Bogoshian, and Irma Russell.
Description: Chicago, Illinois : American Bar Association, [2022] | Includes bibliographical references. | Summary: "A short practice guide for legal professionals to engage in sustainable development in their law practice"—Provided by publisher.
Identifiers: LCCN 2022053728 (print) | LCCN 2022053729 (ebook) | ISBN 9781639051694 (paperback) | ISBN 9781639051700 (ebook)
Subjects: LCSH: Practice of law—Social aspects—United States. | Sustainable development—Philosophy.
Classification: LCC KF300 .D47 2022 (print) | LCC KF300 (ebook) | DDC 340.023/73—dc23/eng/20230207
LC record available at https://lccn.loc.gov/2022053728
LC ebook record available at https://lccn.loc.gov/2022053729

Discounts are available for books ordered in bulk. Special consideration is given to state bars, CLE programs, and other bar-related organizations. Inquire at Book Publishing, ABA Publishing, American Bar Association, 321 N. Clark Street, Chicago, Illinois 60654-7598.

www.shopABA.org

JD: for Kathy, and for Becky, Tess, Ethan, and Ira, and all those in the next generations

IR: for Tom, and for children and grandchildren everywhere

MB: for Robin, our kids, grandkids, family, friends, and fellow Americans

CONTENTS

ABOUT THE AUTHORS

John Dernbach is Commonwealth Professor of Environmental Law and Sustainability at Widener University Commonwealth Law School in Harrisburg, Pennsylvania, and is director of the school's Environmental Law and Sustainability Center. Professor Dernbach has written extensively on sustainable development, climate change, and environmental law. He has chaired or cochaired the ABA Section of Environment, Energy, and Resources (SEER) Climate Change, Sustainable Development, and Ecosystems Committee and is a member of the ABA SEER Climate Change Task Force. He helps lead the Model Laws for Deep Decarbonization Project, a pro bono legal drafting project endorsed by the ABA Section of Environment, Energy, and Resources. He is an elected member of the American Law Institute and the American College of Environmental Lawyers.

Irma Russell is the Edward A. Smith/Missouri Chair at the University of Missouri–Kansas City (UMKC) School of Law. She served as Dean of the Montana School of Law and as Director of the National Energy-Environment Policy Institute at the University of Tulsa. She is a former chair of the ABA SEER and served on the ABA Standing Committee on Professionalism and the ABA Standing Committee on Ethics and Professional Responsibility. In practice, she represented potentially responsible parties, government entities, and lenders on NEPA and CERCLA matters. She was founding Chair of the Environmental Law Section of the Memphis Bar and Chair of the Tennessee Bar Environmental Section. She is an elected member of the American College of Environmental Lawyers and the American Law Institute.

Matt Bogoshian leads the American Manufacturing Communities Collaborative, a successor organization to an Obama administration initiative he helped to lead as Senior Policy Counsel at the U.S. EPA. His range of law experience includes time as a business litigator and general counsel, policy official at the California EPA, consumer and environmental prosecutor, and U.S. Navy JAG Corps officer. His past work includes cofounding the Fourth Sector Group, service on educational and affordable housing boards, writing, podcasting, and teaching environmental and sustainability law at Georgetown University Law Center and at King Hall, University of California, Davis Law School.

ACKNOWLEDGMENTS

This book grows out of the American Bar Association's (ABA's) support for action by lawyers on sustainable development through House of Delegates resolutions adopted in 1991, 2003, and 2013. It also grows out of ABA House of Delegates resolutions endorsing action by lawyers on climate change (2008 and 2019), human dignity (2019), and environmental justice (2021).

All of us are grateful to Kathleen Marion Carr and Manisha Patel for their unconditional support for this project and for helping us navigate the ABA publication process. We are also grateful to Sarah Forbes Orwig and Margrethe Kearney, who converted the manuscript into a book. We deeply appreciate the thoughtful comments of the anonymous peer reviewers, who made this a much better book. We also thank Steve Dujack, editor of the Environmental Law Institute's *Environmental Forum*, who published a much shorter version of this book as an article in 2021 and helped sharpen our thinking.

The authors wish to thank Alex Magnin of *Sustainability Illustrated*, who created and donated his illustrations for this book. Alex created *Sustainability Illustrated* so everybody can learn about sustainability for free. See https://sustainabilityillustrated.com/.

John Dernbach began the work that led to this book when he chaired or cochaired the ABA SEER Climate Change, Sustainable Development, and Ecosystems Committee. He thanks Lynn Bergeson, Frank Friedman, and Maggie Peloso for their early and immediate support and encouragement. Jeremy Wingert provided cheerful secretarial service on the manuscript, and librarian Susan Giusti helped with research. He also thanks the students in his Sustainability Law Practicum classes at Widener Commonwealth Law School in 2020 and 2021, who read draft chapters of this book as part of their coursework and gave helpful feedback.

Irma Russell acknowledges helpful discussions with Professional Responsibility colleagues Professor Meg Reuter and Dean Barb Glesner Fines. She thanks Professors John Ragsdale, J.R. May, and Mary

Christina Wood for their encouragement and insights. She also thanks UMKC law students Anastasia Weston and Christopher Wright.

Matt Bogoshian began the work that led to this book by learning organizing and leadership principles from Marshall Ganz and Leon Panetta. He thanks each of them for their respective work, courage, and supportive conversations over the years. He thanks his many superiors and colleagues in his many jobs who trusted him to take his work in the direction of sustainable development. He also thanks the many who helped sharpen his thinking during the writing of this book, including his 2021 Sustainability Law students at King Hall, University of California, Davis School of Law and his son Zach Bogoshian.

INTRODUCTION

This book is a short practice guide to provide anyone in the legal profession an on-ramp to engage in sustainable development in their particular law practices and communities. It is for lawyers at any stage of their career, and it is not limited to environmental law, energy law, or any other specific legal practice area.

This guide is for you if you went to law school—or are going to law school or considering law school—to help move society and the law profession in a more environmentally, socially, and economically sustainable direction, to protect life on the planet, and to make life better for present and future generations. It is also for you if you did not have this goal in law school but you now want to incorporate sustainable development in your practice.

There is overwhelming evidence we are not meeting the sustainability challenges and opportunities facing our profession, our nation, and the world. While many lawyers are already doing this work, more lawyers need to play a significant role in helping to achieve better outcomes for their clients and communities in ways that accelerate the transition to a sustainable society. We believe that a great many of the nation's 1.3 million lawyers are hungry to do more to advance sustainable development in their own day-to-day work and want to know how to get started. Many are motivated by our inability to more effectively address climate change, social injustice, and pandemics. This guide is intended to enable you to make a contribution, wherever you live or work, in whatever fields of law you are employed, with whatever skills you enjoy using, and with whatever background and experiences you have.

It is increasingly clear that accelerating the transition to sustainable development requires better methods, tools, and choices for lawyers, clients, and citizens alike. It is not enough to ask people generally to move in a more sustainable direction. Across the United States, we make progress toward sustainable development when we are presented with specific and attractive alternatives to unsustainable ways of doing things.[1] Common alternatives to business as usual now include green building, mixed-use zoning, renewable energy, energy efficiency, and the like. Similarly here, this guide is intended to enable you, as a lawyer who wants to make a difference, to help accelerate the transition to sustainable development by providing you with a range of tools, guidelines, and recommendations for your law work and public service. This guide should help you better meet your clients' goals, improve your workplace and profession, influence your communities to make more progress toward sustainable development, and provide you greater personal and professional satisfaction.

Many articles and web stories describe the work of particular lawyers doing this work, and the websites of some law firms describe their sustainability law practice. But the missing element is a relatively short, practical, experience-based guide on how to get started and what to do. This guide is intended to fill that gap.

Some of the raw material for this book was supplied by lawyers who now provide, or for a substantial part of their legal career provided, sustainability-related legal advice to clients. One of us (Dernbach) conducted structured interviews of 26 such lawyers and published the results in the *Denver Law Review* in 2017.[2] Two of us (Dernbach and Bogoshian) participated in a 2021 project with the Reuters news organization surveying how large U.S. law firms use sustainable development in their law practice.[3] One of us (Russell) has devoted years of effort to thinking and writing about the relationship between legal ethics and sustainability in law practice.[4] We have found from these and other experiences that, at its best, sustainable development in law practice is not just a relabeling of traditional environmental law or energy law work or a clever marketing gimmick for law firms. Rather, it provides a lens or perspective for identifying opportunities, options,

1. John C. Dernbach et al., Acting as If Tomorrow Matters: Accelerating the Transition to Sustainability (2012).

2. John C. Dernbach, *Sustainable Development in Law Practice: A Lens for Addressing All Legal Problems*, 95 Denv. L. Rev. 123 (2017). Unless otherwise cited, quotations or summaries of statements from lawyers throughout this book are taken from this article. We are grateful to the *Denver Law Review* for permission to republish portions of that article.

3. Alex Cohen, *We Put These ESG Lawyers to the Test*, Reuters (July 28, 2021), https://www.reuters.com/legal/legalindustry/we-put-these-esg-lawyers-test-2021-07-26/.

4. *See, e.g.*, Ethics and Environmental Practice: A Lawyer's Guide (Irma S. Russell & Vicki J. Wright eds., Am. Bar Ass'n 2017).

and risks for clients that cannot be fully provided in any other way. In addition, that perspective can productively inform any area or type of law practice. We will use interviews from these lawyers and feedback from these law firms frequently in this book.

There is no single route by which people get interested in incorporating sustainable development into their legal work. You may have a lifelong interest in sustainability and sustainability concepts. You may have gone to law school to do this kind of legal work. You may have developed your interest during college or jobs prior to law school. Your interest may have grown out of your work in environmental law, energy law, environmental justice, or human rights law. This interest may be intensifying over time. As one lawyer explains: "As you age, and you become a grandparent, you think about what kind of legacy you and others leave behind for your grandkids." You may be reinventing yourself, your career, or your law practice, or you may be thinking about what to do after retirement. Or you may have been led to sustainability by specific workplace or community experiences involving projects, perspectives, clients, or colleagues that exposed you to sustainable development concepts. These experiences may have fed a sense of dissonance between what you are doing and what you want to do, which is leading you to consider moving your career more in the direction of sustainable development. Whatever your route, this book is intended to provide you tools to get started and accelerate your pace.

This book is not a treatise on sustainable development law. Nor does it present policy or legal recommendations or advice for fostering sustainable development[5] or reducing greenhouse gas emissions.[6] While such resources are helpful for sustainable development in law practice, this book has a different purpose.

This guide is built on three pillars—sustainable development, ethics, and leadership. Sustainable development is a normative conceptual framework for integrating environmental protection with economic development, social well-being, and security in a way that more fully realizes all of them, instead of treating them as inherently opposing or unrelated concepts. It may be one of the most important ideas to

5. *See, e.g.*, GOVERNING FOR SUSTAINABILITY (John C. Dernbach & Scott Schang eds., forthcoming 2022).

6. *See, e.g.*, LEGAL PATHWAYS TO DEEP DECARBONIZATION IN THE UNITED STATES (Michael B. Gerrard & John C. Dernbach eds., 2019).

come out of the 20th century. Sustainable development deserves that claim because it provides an overall framework for humans to live in harmony with nature, rather than at nature's expense, as we have for centuries. Some authors describe it as an idea or principle of the same level of fundamental importance as freedom, equality, and justice.[7]

Sustainable development is one part hard law, several parts soft law, and many parts future law. It is reflected to some extent in legally enforceable public law requirements, or hard law. Our environmental laws are perhaps the most prominent example. In many respects, they have brought us higher quality of life, improvements in public health, and greater protection for ecosystems, even as our economy has grown.

Sustainable development is probably reflected to a greater extent in soft law, meaning instruments that have some legal effect but are not legally binding or enforceable on their own terms. These include norms that grow out of international conferences or institutions (e.g., Sustainable Development Goals, discussed in Chapter 1); various sustainability certification programs (e.g., green building, forestry); and a variety of other norms or programs like voluntary corporate reporting programs and standards for sustainability and climate change that are known collectively as Environmental, Social, and Governance (ESG). ESG is also discussed in more detail later in this book. Many of these soft law instruments will likely at some point become hard law—as the basis for drafting statutes or regulations, through incorporation into legally binding contracts, and by other means.

A great deal of additional law for sustainable development remains to be enacted and implemented. This includes laws that drive economic development in more sustainable ways as well as more effective and durable legal regimes to address climate change; to prevent and manage pandemics; and to protect biodiversity, international security, and human rights.

The second pillar in this guide is ethics. Lawyers wishing to integrate sustainable development into their law practice tend to have a deeply held moral or ethical perspective, which they strive to apply with integrity and wisdom. Professional ethics also matter. Lawyers need to know not only what the laws and rules expressly require or

7. Klaus Bosselmann, The Principle of Sustainability: Transforming Law and Governance 57 (2008).

prohibit; they also need to understand what conduct the rules permit and the circumstances and professional culture that inform lawyer decision-making. The role of lawyers in our legal system is multidimensional. A lawyer plays, or should play, three related roles: "a representative of clients, an officer of the legal system and a public citizen having special responsibility for the quality of justice."[8] As we will discuss throughout this book, each of these roles is critical for sustainable development lawyers.

The third and final pillar is leadership. Even when lawyers gain a better understanding about the meaning of sustainable development, how to apply it, and the legal and ethical obligations for doing so, lawyers must become leaders in making the systemic changes we need to produce a sustainable society. Understanding the emerging field of systems leadership, becoming a practitioner of systems leadership, and helping to improve our legal and societal systems through the application of systems leadership are key elements to this third pillar of the book.

Lawyers have played significant leadership roles in earlier movements. At the founding of our country, Thomas Jefferson, John Adams, and James Madison were all lawyers. In the 1800s, lawyers applied their legal skills to help abolish slavery. In the 1920s, lawyers helped achieve women's suffrage. In the 1950s and 1960s, lawyers like Thurgood Marshall helped to desegregate schools and establish civil, voting, and housing rights in federal law. In the late 1960s and 1970s, lawyers used their legal skills to create a whole new field of environmental law. Ruth Bader Ginsburg and other lawyers played a formative role in strengthening the rights of women. It is time that lawyers apply this accumulated knowledge to help lead the movement for a sustainable society.

This book is divided in two broad parts that together provide an on-ramp for this work. The first four chapters of this guide provide a foundation for the use of sustainable development in law practice. Chapter 1 provides an overview of the history of the sustainable development framework, emphasizing the centrality of integrated decision-making. Chapter 2 describes in more detail the basic principles lawyers need to know before applying sustainable development in law practice. Chapter 3 explains the lawyer's ethical duty to clients and society to

8. Model Rules of Pro. Conduct, Preamble, para. [1] (Am. Bar Ass'n 2020).

apply sustainability. It focuses on three fundamental principles of lawyering: compliance with and respect for the law, serving legitimate client interests, and advancing legal reform to serve the public good. In Chapter 4, we explain how the sustainable development framework is already being applied in law practice. The remaining chapters build on this foundation, showing how you can make a difference by applying the sustainable development framework. Chapter 5 shows how to get started on sustainability leadership in the law, and Chapter 6 explains how to give effective advice on sustainable development. Chapters 7, 8, and 9 explain and illustrate the use of systems leadership in three different aspects of sustainability law work: in client counseling (Chapter 7), in making the law office more sustainable (Chapter 8), and in the community (Chapter 9). Chapter 10 describes the rewards and frustrations of sustainability work in law practice. Finally, Chapter 11 addresses the future of sustainable development in law practice.

We do not guarantee one way to successfully approach each client or leadership situation on sustainable development. Sustainable development is a relatively new legal perspective, one that demands practice, patience, persistence, and great attention to what clients and communities actually want and need. As you will see in the ensuing chapters, best practices for sustainable development in law practice are a work in progress, and leadership matters. This guide aims to help you on your journey and succeed in making your goals a reality.

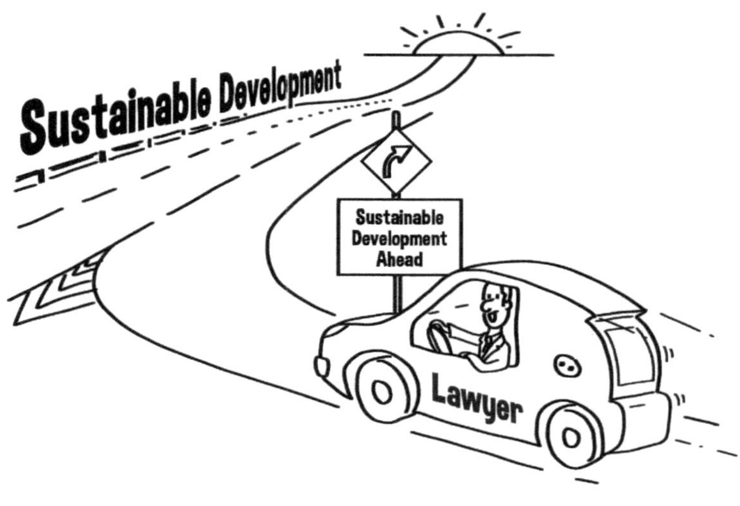

Foundation

1

A Brief History of Sustainable Development

A lawyer doing sustainable development work must have a basic understanding of what sustainable development actually means. To do this work is to be part of a large and growing community that includes not only other lawyers but also sustainability professionals in a wide variety of other fields in the United States and around the globe. This community includes engineers, architects, planners, educators, scientists, technology developers, corporate leaders, government officials, elected leaders, and activists. Being an effective part of this community requires a basic understanding of what sustainable development means.

This chapter provides a brief history of the term "sustainable development," which in our experience is necessary to understand what it means. This chapter also explains what sustainable development is not. Our objective here is to sharpen your ability to apply the concept and enable you to respond effectively to inevitable pushback coming from some quarters when applying its principles. We are well aware that the term "sustainable development" is fraught with misunderstanding, disagreement over its meaning, and even cynicism about its relevance and value. We are also aware of a wide variety of criticisms of even a well-defined sustainable development. This chapter provides an overview of some of the most basic criticisms, along with answers to these criticisms.

1. Old Model for Human Progress: Development

Although many use the term "sustainability" as a substitute for "sustainable development," the original and best term to use is sustainable development because it is more historically accurate. To understand what sustainable development means, it is first necessary to understand what the term "development" means. Americans, including American lawyers, tend to understand development in terms of some kind of economic development, as in a housing development or an industrial development project. But that narrow meaning of "development" does not capture what the term came to mean in the international context as a precursor to the term "sustainable development."[1]

From an international perspective, "[t]he satisfaction of human needs and aspirations is the major objective of development."[2] "For most practitioners and theorists," says Rumu Sarkar, an international development lawyer, "the overall objectives of alleviating poverty and human suffering and of improving the human condition more generally are the desired end product of the development process."[3] Use of the term "development" as a means of improving the human condition can be traced at least as far back as the end of World War II, when the United States, United Kingdom, and other countries helped create an international legal system to prevent another world war or economic depression from happening again.[4] The idea was to make sure that basic human needs were met, and the focal point of that effort

1. When we use "sustainability" in this book, we use it as a synonym for "sustainable development."

2. World Commission on Environment and Development, Our Common Future 54 (1987).

3. Rumu Sarkar, International Development Law: Rule of Law, Human Rights, and Global Finance xvi (Oxford University Press 2009).

4. This summary of the origins of development is taken from John C. Dernbach, *Sustainable Development as a Framework for National Governance*, 49 Case W. Res. L. Rev. 1, 8–24 (1998). *See also* Elizabeth Borgwardt, A New Deal for the World: America's Vision for Human Rights (2005); Stephen C. Schlesinger, Acts of Creation: The Founding of the United Nations (2003).

was human development, or simply "development." At the time, they understood human development to require three basic things: economic development, social development or human rights, and peace and security.

This understanding of development contains an echo of President Franklin Roosevelt's famous 1941 State of the Union address to Congress, which has come to be known as the Four Freedoms speech. In this speech, which is easily among the most significant of his presidency, Roosevelt said, "[W]e look forward to a world founded upon four essential human freedoms" for each person anywhere in a not-too-distant world—(1) "freedom of speech and expression," (2) "freedom of every person to worship God in his own way," (3) "freedom from want—which . . . means economic understandings which will secure to every nation a healthy peacetime life for its inhabitants," and (4) "freedom from fear—which . . . means . . . that no nation will be in a position to commit an act of physical aggression against any neighbor. . . ."[5] These freedoms track the core elements of development—social development or human rights (freedom of speech and worship), economic development (freedom from want), and peace and security (freedom from fear).

These three components of conventional development should be mutually reinforcing. Social and economic development are interdependent; healthy and educated workers in legal systems that respect basic human rights tend to be more productive, and economic development provides the income and capital necessary for the food, water, schools, and hospitals that people need to thrive. We do not ordinarily think of development as including peace and security, but the generation that came out of World War II—and all too many since then—know full well how difficult it is to run a business or go to school when there are tanks in the streets or soldiers shooting from nearby rooftops. The Russian invasion of Ukraine makes crystal clear the importance of peace and security to development.

The objectives of this broader understanding of "development," as the Four Freedoms speech indicates, are human freedom, opportunity, and quality of life. Economist Amartya Sen explains development as

5. Transcript of President Franklin Roosevelt's Annual Message (Four Freedoms) to Congress (1941), U.S. Nat'l Archives & Records Admin., https://www.archives.gov/milestone-documents/president-franklin-roosevelts-annual-message-to-congress.

a process that enlarges individual freedom.[6] And, it was believed, these objectives are impossible to achieve without economic development, social development (or human rights), and peace and security. A great many international institutions and agreements were established or adopted to further this framework: the United Nations (peace and security), the International Monetary Fund (economic development), the World Trade Organization (economic development), the World Bank (also known as the International Bank for Reconstruction and Development) (economic and social development), and numerous human rights treaties (social development).

Since World War II, development has succeeded in many ways. More people have a higher standard of living now than at any other time in human history. Between 1961 and 2019, annual global gross domestic product (GDP), adjusted for inflation, grew from about $12 trillion to more than $87 trillion.[7] U.S. GDP, adjusted for inflation, grew from just under $2.3 trillion in 1950 to just over $19 trillion in 2019.[8] Although the coronavirus pandemic has reduced economic growth, the contraction is only a fraction of the overall economic growth since World War II.

Similarly, for many facets of social development, there have been distinct improvements. Since 1950, life expectancy in the United States, for example, has grown from the low 60s to the high 70s, while life expectancy in China has grown from under 40 to the high 70s.[9] Although there are still significant differences in education among countries, people overall are better educated than ever, whether measured by decline in the illiteracy rate, number of years in school, or improved learning outcomes. Better education both predicts and is required for economic growth.[10]

---

6. Amartya Sen, Development as Freedom (1999); *see also* Koen De Feyter, World Development Law: Sharing Responsibility for Development 32 (2001).

7. *Gross Domestic Product*, Worldometer, https://www.worldometers.info/gdp/ (last visited June 1, 2020).

8. Kimberly Amadeo, *US GDP by Year, Compared to Recessions and Events*, The Balance (Mar. 13, 2020), https://www.thebalance.com/us-gdp-by-year-3305543.

9. Max Roser, Esteban Ortiz-Ospina & Hannah Ritchie, *Life Expectancy*, Our World in Data, https://ourworldindata.org/life-expectancy (last revised Oct. 2019).

10. Max Roser & Esteban Ortiz-Ospina, *Global Education*, Our World in Data, https://ourworldindata.org/global-education (last visited June 25, 2020).

Terrorism and many regional wars and other conflicts, as well as various nuclear and other threats, rightfully get public attention, but there has been no third world war. World War II, it should be recalled, caused 35 to 60 million military and civilian deaths.[11] No other subsequent conflict or terrorist event comes even close to that. In that sense, there has been improvement in peace and security.

This understanding of development also helps flag problems that need attention. Freedom House, a nongovernmental organization, issues an annual report on freedom and human rights around the world. Between 2005 and 2021, it found, the percentage of people living in "free" countries declined from 46.0 percent to 20.3 percent, while the percentage of people living in countries labeled "not free" or "partly free" increased from 54.0 percent to 79.7 percent.[12] Across the globe, Freedom House said in its 2022 report, there have been "16 years of democratic decline."[13] It added: "The United States has fallen below its traditional peers on key democratic indicators, including executive elections, freedom from improper political influence, and equal treatment of minority groups."[14]

For poverty alleviation, a core objective of conventional development, the story is also complicated. At least until the COVID-19 pandemic, global poverty had declined. The number of people living in extreme poverty fell by more than a billion (from 1.9 billion to 730 million) between 1990 and 2015.[15] A person with an income of less than $1.90 per day in 2011 purchasing power is considered to be in extreme poverty.[16] Still, there were about 730 million such people in 2015. The COVID-19 crisis, however, caused a global increase in extreme poverty for the first time in two decades, pushing as many as

---

11. *World War II, 1939–45: Costs of the War: Killed, Wounded, Prisoners, or Missing*, Encyc. Britannica, https://www.britannica.com/event/World-War-II/Costs-of-the-war (last visited June 25, 2020).

12. Sarah Repucci & Amy Slipowitz, Freedom House, Freedom in the World 2022: The Global Expansion of Authoritarian Rule 4 (2022).

13. *Id.* at 2.

14. *Id.* at 9.

15. Max Roser & Esteban Ortiz-Ospina, *Global Extreme Poverty*, Our World in Data, https://ourworldindata.org/extreme-poverty (last visited Mar. 4, 2021).

16. Int'l Bank for Reconstr. & Dev./The World Bank, Poverty and Shared Prosperity 2018: Piecing Together the Poverty Puzzle 1 (2018), https://openknowledge.worldbank.org/bitstream/handle/10986/30418/9781464813306.pdf.

150 million more people into extreme poverty.[17] The Russian invasion of Ukraine appears likely to increase poverty and hardship by interrupting global supply chains. Most of us, looking back over the past 75 years, would nonetheless say there has been progress on development, although there have been reversals on human rights and democracy as well as poverty alleviation. But decades ago, it was also becoming clear that progress in development came at growing costs in environmental degradation and human inequality.[18] Even then, those who supported development justified it on the grounds that its benefits outweighed its costs. That justification does not hold up.

Deep poverty, inequality, and widespread environmental degradation are weakening, undermining, and even threatening to overcome the progress that has come with conventional development. Major contributing factors are not only the economic growth described earlier, but also unprecedented increases in population. The global human population has tripled since shortly after the end of World War II, from about 2.5 billion in 1950[19] to more than 7.8 billion in 2022.[20] U.S. population has more than doubled, from about 151 million in 1950[21] to more than 332 million in 2022.[22]

Environmental degradation causes or contributes to much human poverty and injustice. The poor tend to live in the most polluted and resource-limited places. But while environmental degradation causes

17. Press Release, The World Bank, COVID-19 to Add as Many as 150 Million Extreme Poor by 2021 (Oct. 7, 2020), https://www.worldbank.org/en/news/press-release/2020/10/07/covid-19-to-add-as-many-as-150-million-extreme-poor-by-2021#:~:text=The%20COVID%2D19%20pandemic%20is,severity%20of%20the%20economic%20contraction.

18. U.N. Dep't of Econ. & Social Affairs, World Social Report 2020: Inequality in a Rapidly Changing World (2020), https://www.un.org/development/desa/dspd/wp-content/uploads/sites/22/2020/02/World-Social-Report2020-FullReport.pdf (explaining that the four major driving forces behind growing inequality are technological innovation, climate change, urbanization, and international migration).

19. *Historical Estimates of World Population*, U.S. Census Bureau, https://www.census.gov/data/tables/time-series/demo/international-programs/historical-est-worldpop.html (last revised Dec. 16, 2021).

20. *U.S. and World Population Clock*, U.S. Census Bureau, https://www.census.gov/popclock/ (last visited Mar. 1, 2022).

21. *A Look at the 1940 Census* 4, U.S. Census Bureau, https://www.census.gov/newsroom/cspan/1940census/CSPAN_1940slides.pdf (last visited June 1, 2020).

22. *U.S. and World Population Clock*, *supra* note 20.

and contributes to much poverty and injustice, not all poverty and injustices are caused by environmental problems.

The landmark 1987 report of the World Commission on Environment and Development, *Our Common Future*, explained and documented these troubling trends in considerable detail—trends that sadly have accelerated since it was published.[23] The report also explained the relationship between environment and development: "Environment and development are not separate challenges; they are inexorably linked. Development cannot subsist upon a deteriorating environmental resource base; the environment cannot be protected when growth leaves out of account the costs of environmental destruction."[24]

A great many subsequent books, reports, and articles update and amplify *Our Common Future*'s description of deteriorating environmental and social conditions. We are not recounting them here; you can simply read or watch the news.

The following table summarizes the insufficiency of the conventional development (or, simply, development) framework for making progress. As you can see, progress under this framework necessarily comes with a large price.

Conventional Development Framework

Progress	Price of Progress
—Economic development —Social development/human rights/ healthy communities —Peace and security	—Environment and natural resources degraded —Living people harmed by pollution and inequality —Future generations harmed by pollution and inequality

2. New Model for Human Progress: Sustainable Development

To correct two of many basic limitations in the conventional development framework—growing environmental degradation and extreme poverty—nations of the world committed to *sustainable* development.

23. World Comm'n on Env't & Dev., Our Common Future (1987).
24. *Id.* at 37.

They first did so at the U.N. Conference on Environment and Development (Earth Summit) in 1992. These nations, including the United States, approved an ambitious plan for sustainable development and a set of 27 principles, known as the Rio Declaration, to guide their efforts.[25] The central action principle in the Rio Declaration is integrated decision-making—making decisions that further both development and environmental protection.[26] Other principles include intergenerational equity and the use of precaution toward the environment when scientific uncertainty exists.[27]

Essentially, sustainable development redefines progress. This is a big deal and has enormous implications for how we act if we take it seriously. It is not enough to make progress on the basic components of conventional development; it is also essential to protect and conserve natural resources and the environment. Sustainable development occurs when multiple goals—peace and security, economic development, social development, and environmental and natural resources protection and conservation—are achieved at the same time. It is not just about the environment and equity; it is about achieving all of these goals. If that is done, then we can continually reduce any kind of "price of progress." That is why there is no "price of progress" in the following table.

Sustainable Development Framework

Progress
—Peace and security —Equitable economic development —Social development/human rights/healthy communities —Environmental and natural resources protection and conservation

Nations of the world have reaffirmed this commitment to sustainable development rather than conventional development many times

25. U.N. Conf. on Env't & Dev., Agenda 21 (1992), https://sustainabledevelopment.un.org/content/documents/Agenda21.pdf; *Rio Declaration on Environment and Development*, Principles 3–4, 8, U.N. Conf. on Env't & Dev., U.N. Doc. A/CONF.151/26 (Vol. I), annex I (Aug. 12, 1992) [hereinafter *Rio Declaration*].

26. John C. Dernbach, *Achieving Sustainable Development: The Centrality and Multiple Facets of Integrated Decisionmaking*, 10 Ind. J. Glob. Legal Stud. 247 (2003).

27. *Rio Declaration*, Principles 3 & 15, *supra* note 25.

since then, perhaps most notably in 2015, when, in a U.N. General Assembly Resolution, they endorsed 17 Sustainable Development Goals (SDGs), nearly all of which are to be achieved by 2030.[28] The United States took an active role in the development and endorsement of those goals.[29] The SDGs are the current international action plan for making human progress. The 17 goals range broadly and include ending poverty and hunger, equitably reducing greenhouse gas emissions, and achieving justice and good governance. These 17 goals include 169 specific targets. For example, Goal 11 ("sustainable cities and communities") is to be implemented by achieving ten targets for 2030. These targets include

- ensuring "access for all to adequate, safe and affordable housing and basic services,"
- providing "access to safe, affordable, accessible and sustainable transport systems for all," and
- reducing "the adverse per capita environmental impact of cities."

In all of the goals and targets, the world's nations stated, "we are setting out a supremely ambitious and transformational vision." They also recognized that "each country has primary responsibility for its own economic and social development"[30] and that implementation within individual countries will take "into account different national realities, capacities and levels of development" as well as "national policies and priorities."[31] The resolution encourages countries to publish voluntary national reviews of their progress toward the SDGs.[32] These voluntary national reviews are available online.[33]

To assist the SDG implementation effort and encourage comparable reporting on outcomes among countries, the U.N. General Assembly adopted a resolution in 2017 that sets out indicators for measuring

---

28. G.A. Res. 70/1, Transforming Our World: The 2030 Agenda for Sustainable Development (Oct. 21, 2015) [hereinafter Transforming Our World].

29. Anthony F. Pipa & Kaysie Brown, *American Leadership on the Sustainable Development Goals*, BROOKINGS (Oct. 14, 2019), https://www.brookings.edu/blog/up-front/2019/10/14/american-leadership-on-the-sustainable-development-goals/.

30. Transforming Our World, *supra* note 28, ¶ 41.

31. *Id.* ¶ 21.

32. *Id.* ¶ 79.

33. *Voluntary National Reviews*, U.N. HIGH-LEVEL POL. FORUM ON SUSTAINABLE DEV., https://sustainabledevelopment.un.org/vnrs/ (last visited Apr. 7, 2022).

performance in achieving the SDGs and urges countries to report progress using these indicators.[34] In addition, the United Nations maintains a searchable database concerning the SDG indicators[35] and produces an annual report on global progress in meeting them.[36]

In addition to national governments, many cities, people, and other organizations—in the United States and around the world—are working to achieve the SDGs, including Los Angeles, Houston, and Baltimore.[37] The U.N. Global Compact, a voluntary nonprofit organization that describes itself as the "world's largest corporate sustainability initiative," with more than 8,000 business participants,[38] provides businesses with information, tools, and resources to participate in the achievement of the SDGs.[39] Colleges and universities throughout the world are implementing the SDGs; there is even an annual ranking of the top universities.[40] Many local governments have incorporated the SDGs into their goal setting and governance activities.[41] These goals also suggest a wide variety of actions that need to be taken to

---

34. G.A. Res. 71/13, Work of the Statistical Commission Pertaining to the 2030 Agenda for Sustainable Development, ¶¶ 1, 6 & 11 (July 10, 2017).

35. *Sustainable Development Goals: SDG Indicators Database*, U.N. DEP'T OF ECON. & SOCIAL AFFAIRS, https://unstats.un.org/sdgs/indicators/database/ (last visited Apr. 7, 2022).

36. *See, e.g.*, U.N. Secretary-General, *Progress towards the Sustainable Development Goals*, U.N. Doc. E/2021/58 (Apr. 30, 2021), https://undocs.org/en/E/2021/58. When the SDGs overlap with other international agreements, such as the U.N. Framework Convention on Climate Change, emissions reductions under the Convention are reported for the SDGs. *Id.* at 20–21.

37. *See* PROMOTING THE SUSTAINABLE DEVELOPMENT GOALS IN NORTH AMERICAN CITIES: CASE STUDIES & BEST PRACTICES IN THE SCIENCE OF SUSTAINABILITY INDICATORS (David B. Abraham & Seema D. Iyer eds., 2021).

38. U.N. GLOB. COMPACT, GUIDE TO CORPORATE SUSTAINABILITY: SHAPING A SUSTAINABLE FUTURE 6 (2014), https://d306pr3pise04h.cloudfront.net/docs/publications%2FUN_Global_Compact_Guide_to_Corporate_Sustainability.pdf.

39. *17 Goals to Transform Our World*, U.N. GLOB. COMPACT, https://www.unglobalcompact.org/sdgs/17-global-goals (last visited Apr. 7, 2022).

40. *Top Universities in the World for Global Impact*, TIMES HIGHER EDUC.: THE STUDENT (Apr. 21, 2021), https://www.timeshighereducation.com/student/best-universities/top-universities-world-global-impact.

41. Anthony F. Pipa & Max Bouchet, *Ensuring the Durability of Local Commitments to the SDGs*, BROOKINGS (June 18, 2021), https://www.brookings.edu/blog/up-front/2021/06/18/ensuring-the-durability-of-local-commitments-to-the-sdgs/. *See also* SUSTAINABLE DEV. SOLS. NETWORK, A PATHWAY TO SUSTAINABLE AMERICAN CITIES: A GUIDE TO IMPLEMENTING THE SDGS (2019), https://irp-cdn.multiscreensite.com/be6d1d56/files/uploaded/190123-2019-us-cities-guide-INT.pdf.

accelerate sustainable development in the United States at the federal, state, and local levels and in private governance.[42]

The SDGs further the conceptual framework for sustainable development by providing a set of targets and indicators for all countries, whether developing or developed, to identify, prioritize, measure, and report progress toward each goal. Implemented properly, the SDGs reinforce each other; progress toward one goal can and should further progress on other goals. That, of course, is the point of integrated decision-making.

For businesses, particularly but not exclusively publicly traded corporations, an increasingly central part of sustainable development falls under the heading of ESG (Environmental, Social, and Governance). Many businesses use ESG criteria to guide their actions on environmental, human rights, labor, climate change, diversity, and other issues. Some of these criteria are in the form of voluntary sustainability standards developed by the International Standards Organization,[43] the Sustainability Accounting Standards Board,[44] and other entities. Some public reporting standards for corporate sustainability activities apply broadly to sustainable development, and some focus only on climate change. The latter include the U.N. Global Compact, the Carbon Disclosure Project,[45] the Global Reporting Initiative,[46] and the Task Force on Climate-Related Financial Disclosures,[47] among others. While adherence to these criteria is primarily voluntary, investor pressure has begun to drive more ambitious corporate sustainable development goals, including but not limited to reduced or net-zero greenhouse gas emissions, as well as greater transparency (i.e., honesty) in reporting

42. Governing for Sustainability (John C. Dernbach & Scott Schang eds., forthcoming 2022); John C. Dernbach & Scott Schang eds., *Making America a Better Place for All: Sustainable Development Recommendations for the Biden Administration*, 51 Env't L. Rep. (Env't L. Inst.) 10310 (2021).

43. *Developing Sustainably*, Int'l Org. for Standardization, https://www.iso.org/developing-sustainably.html (last visited Apr. 7, 2022).

44. Sustainability Acct. Standards Bd., https://www.sasb.org/ (last visited Apr. 7, 2022).

45. Carbon Disclosure Project, https://www.cdp.net/en (last visited Apr. 7, 2022).

46. Glob. Reporting Initiative, https://www.globalreporting.org/ (last visited Apr. 7, 2022).

47. Task Force on Climate-Related Fin. Disclosures, https://www.fsb-tcfd.org/ (last visited Apr. 7, 2022).

of corporate performance. Investor interest in ESG marks a departure from a more traditional view that corporate performance should be measured primarily in financial terms. ESG measures corporate performance according to sustainability's "triple bottom line," which includes not only economic but also environmental and social performance. Interestingly, there is considerable data that ESG commitments improve a company's financial performance.[48]

Sustainable development, thus understood, is the internationally accepted framework, endorsed by the United States, for maintaining and improving the human condition. It is a guide for action, including action by lawyers.[49]

3. Answers to Common Misconceptions and Criticisms of Sustainable Development

This account provides a way of understanding what sustainable development is not. Recognizing these (and other) misunderstandings is necessary to stay focused and respond effectively to criticisms.

Sustainable development is not an oxymoron. Some people balk at the use of the word "development" in the term "sustainable development" because they think development means conventional economic development and thus see development as necessarily and inevitably environmentally damaging. They thus mistakenly conclude that "sustainable" and "development" are contradictory terms. But sustainable development is not a description of current affairs; it is a decision-making framework for transforming human progress.

Sustainable development is not yet realized in a body of law, like environmental law or natural resources law. While some laws can properly be called sustainable development laws, they are not the same as the concept itself. Sustainable development is a normative framework, not a set of existing laws. In addition to being a framework for establishing objectives to make life better for this and future

---

48. *See, e.g.*, Gunnar Friede et al., *ESG and Financial Performance: Aggregated Evidence from More Than 2000 Empirical Studies*, 5 J. Sustainable Fin. & Inv. 210 (2015).

49. John C. Dernbach & Federico Cheever, *Sustainable Development and Its Discontents*, 4 Transnat'l Env't L. 247 (2015).

generations, sustainable development is about how we should approach decision-making.

Sustainable development is not another term for big government or environmental regulation. Environmental regulation is an important tool in protecting the environment but, at its best, tends to prevent or deter only the worst environmental practices. So it is necessary but not sufficient for sustainable development. Sustainable development is broader in scope and has a greater emphasis on achieving positive and regenerative outcomes. Sustainable development cannot be achieved by preventing bad outcomes or by environmental regulation alone; it requires a great variety of legal tools, including removal of legal barriers and the application of new and existing economic development tools. In fact, sustainable development requires the active and constructive participation of all sectors of society, including not only government but also citizens and nongovernmental organizations as well as business and industry. Public–private partnerships are a common way of making progress toward sustainable development.

Sustainable development is not another term for environmentalism or environmental protection. To be sure, protecting the environment is foundational to sustainable development. Without a livable environment, sustainable development is impossible. But sustainable development is about more than environmental protection; it is also about fostering human well-being at the same time.

Sustainable development is not simply about "balancing" the environmental, economic, and social aspects of a proposal, in which each inevitably gets half (more or less) of what they could otherwise get, and at the expense of the others. Sustainable development is not a zero-sum approach. Rather, it is about making as much progress as possible on each aspect in each decision and, by doing so, unlocking opportunities. Perhaps the ultimate test of such decisions, as economist Kate Raworth states, is whether they foster "human prosperity in a flourishing web of life."[50]

Sustainable development is not another term for sustainable growth or sustained economic growth. Economic development is part of sustainable development, but sustainable development is a framework for integrated decision-making, not simply realizing profits or

50. Kate Raworth, Doughnut Economics: Seven Ways to Think Like a 21st Century Economist 47 (2017).

consistently generating economic growth. More basically, the ultimate objective of sustainable development is human well-being; economic development is an important (but not the only) means of achieving that.

Being able to respond to confusion about what sustainable development means also includes being able to respond to criticisms of the SDGs—including claims that there are too many targets and that the SDGs themselves are too ambitious. Significantly, the SDGs are the successor to the Millennium Development Goals, adopted in 2000 and intended to be achieved by 2015.[51] The Millennium Development Goals were directed primarily at reducing poverty around the world; the SDGs address poverty as well as the broader range of sustainable development issues. The final U.N. report on the Millennium Development Goals found that, while most of the goals were not fully achieved, they "produced the most successful anti-poverty movement in history."[52] Similarly, the concerted international effort to implement the SDGs is likely, at a minimum, to produce more progress toward sustainable development by 2030 than would occur without the SDGs. Another criticism of the SDGs is that they create 17 different "silos," goals that can be achieved without reference to the others, and thus undermine integrated decision-making. The SDGs themselves, however, are replete with reference to their interdependence; that is, progress toward one goal should result in progress toward other goals. That said, there is a distinct risk that some SDGs, particularly those involving environmental protection, will be given much lower priority. But greater attention to environmental protection has been a challenge with sustainable development since its inception; improving environmental outcomes will require more persistent and effective effort.

Finally, sustainable development is not a clever policy fad that will inevitably be replaced by something better, or at least different. Instead, sustainable development is a framework that needs to be realized more fully and completely over time. The transition to

---

51. G.A. Res. 55/2, United Nations Millennium Declaration (Sept. 18, 2000).

52. United Nations, The Millennium Development Goals Report 2015 (2017), https://www.un.org/millenniumgoals/2015_MDG_Report/pdf/MDG%20 2015%20rev%20(July%201).pdf. *See also* John W. McArthur & Krista Rasmussen, *Change of Pace: Accelerations and Advances during the Millennium Development Goal Era*, 105 World Dev. 132 (2018) (analyzing goals and groups of countries for which improvements did and did not accelerate).

a decarbonized economy, for example, will almost certainly take decades. Unfortunately, some mistakenly consider "resilience" as a concept to replace sustainable development as an organizing framework for human progress. That idea is understandable but wrong. Resilience is a means of surviving system shocks rather than maintaining and improving human quality of life. As the adverse impacts of climate change grow, so do calls for greater resilience, for example, in where and how things are built. And more recently, with the COVID-19 pandemic, it has become clearer that institutions need to become more resilient by planning to withstand such social disruption. But unlike sustainable development, resilience is not tethered to any kind of normative framework for determining what broader outcomes a sustainable society should seek. Properly understood, resilience is part of sustainable development. Sustainable development provides a way of integrating resilience to address relevant threats as a part of public and private decision-making, whatever the threat. We need to prepare for the impacts of climate change, for example, but we must also reduce greenhouse gas emissions in a way that provides a just transition. The need for the sustainable development framework is not going away; to the contrary, the need is growing. Lawyers need to help lead this effort.

2

Basic Principles for Applying Sustainable Development

In Chapter 1, we explained the history of sustainable development as a way of understanding what the term means. This chapter translates this history into three practical principles for lawyers to understand and apply the term. Sustainable development, after all, is not a theory; it is a guide to action.

1. The Objective of Sustainable Development Is to Improve the Lives of Each Person in Present and Future Generations

The goals of sustainable development include the same goals as conventional development—human freedom, opportunity, and quality of life. Sustainable development focuses on these goals for both present and future generations. The very first principle in the Rio Declaration makes this clear: "Human beings are at the center of concerns for sustainable development. They are entitled to a healthy and productive life in harmony with nature."[1] The most widely quoted definition of sustainable development, from *Our Common Future*, also makes this clear: it is "development that meets the needs of the present without compromising the ability of future generations to meet their own needs."[2] As noted in Chapter 1, economist Kate Raworth describes sustainable development as "human prosperity in a flourishing web of life."[3] It is, we now recognize, difficult if not impossible to foster human well-being without also protecting and restoring the environment. As the National Research Council stated in 2011:

Sustainability is based on a simple and long-recognized factual premise:

> Everything that humans require for their survival and well-being depends, directly or indirectly, on the natural environment. . . .The environment provides the air we breathe, the water we drink, and the food we eat. It defines in fundamental ways the communities in which we live and is the source for renewable and nonrenewable resources on which civilization depends. Our health and wellbeing, our economy, and our security all require a high quality environment.[4]

Sustainable development is also based on concern for the well-being of *each* human. The call in the Declaration of Independence for the equal right of all people to "life, liberty, and the pursuit of happiness" is an important expression of this concern.[5] It is not enough that some human beings, or even a great majority of us, do well. Extreme poverty, which environmental degradation often causes or worsens, is an example of something we should not want for anyone. This notion of universality is expressed throughout the Sustainable Development Goals (SDGs). For example, Goal 3 is "Ensure healthy

1. *Rio Declaration on Environment and Development*, Principle 1, U.N. Conf. on Env't & Dev., U.N. Doc. A/CONF.151/26 (Vol. I), annex I (Aug. 12, 1992) [hereinafter *Rio Declaration*].

2. World Comm'n on Env't & Dev., Our Common Future 43 (1987).

3. Kate Raworth, Doughnut Economics: Seven Ways to Think Like a 21st Century Economist 47 (2017).

4. Nat'l Rsch. Council, Sustainability and the U.S. EPA 15 (2011) (citation omitted).

5. Jon Meacham, The Soul of America: The Battle for Our Better Angels (2018); Danielle S. Allen, Our Declaration: A Reading of the Declaration of Independence in Defense of Equality (2014).

lives and promote well-being for all at all ages."[6] This universality also applies to future generations. Indeed, sustainable development is in response to the widely observed tendency of the present generation to prioritize its needs and wants over those of future generations. This concern for the well-being of each human also contrasts with a variety of economic and philosophical approaches that, roughly speaking, are focused on overall or aggregate well-being, or well-being for some and not others.

As noted in Chapter 1, one measure of human well-being is human freedom. Sustainable development is needed to protect and enhance freedom for this and future generations. Human freedom can be understood in two ways—positive freedoms, which are "freedoms to" do certain things, and negative freedoms, which are "freedoms from" other things.[7] Ensuring both positive and negative freedoms for each person is essential to effectuating sustainable development's objective of making life better for each person in this and future generations.

Some aspects of the first kind of freedom, "positive freedom," are familiar. We want to say what we want, work where we want, live where we want, and raise a family if we want. We want, in short, to be in charge of our lives, to exercise our will to make our own choices.[8] But that positive freedom does not exist in the abstract; positive freedom requires the existence of structures, institutions, and environmental qualities that equip us with capabilities to make these choices; they give us the "freedom to" thrive. That is, in order for each of us as individuals to have a minimal amount of agency and choice, we need to be healthy and educated, to have a place to live and a decent job, and to live in a clean environment.[9] These are basic enabling conditions for a "good" quality of life.

---

6. G.A. Res. 70/1, Transforming Our World: The 2030 Agenda for Sustainable Development, Goal 3 (Oct. 21, 2015) [hereinafter Transforming Our World].

7. Isaiah Berlin, Two Concepts of Liberty (1958).

8. Isaiah Berlin explained positive freedom this way: "I wish my life and decisions to depend on myself, not on external forces of whatever kind. I wish to be the instrument of my own, not of other men's, acts of will." Isaiah Berlin, *Two Concepts of Liberty*, *in* Four Essays on Liberty 15, 22–23 (1969).

9. *What's America's Purpose* podcast, episode 2 (May 8, 2020), http://whatsamericaspurpose.com/episode-2-americas-maestro-of-organizing-marshall-ganz/ (Marshall Ganz explaining his interpretation of positive freedom in an American context).

"Negative freedoms," in contrast, are "freedoms from" infringements on our personal liberties by others, particularly the government.[10] The rights recognized in the U.S. Bill of Rights illustrate these kinds of negative freedoms—freedom from government interfering with our individual liberties. The Four Freedoms that Roosevelt described include two of these negative freedoms—freedom of speech and religion. We also want "freedom from" arbitrary uses of governmental power without due process, from unreasonable governmental searches and seizures, and the like. Ensuring negative freedom also requires structures and institutions that equip us with capabilities to enjoy these protections. These are essential "freedoms from" government actions that prevent us from exercising our own will to live the lives we want to live.

When Roosevelt spoke of "freedom from want" and "freedom from fear," however, he was not speaking about freedom from government actions. He was speaking about positive freedoms and securing conditions that enable people to make meaningful life choices for their health, wealth, and security. In a sustainable development context, a clean and healthy environment as well as adequate resources for everyone are basic enabling conditions for quality of life. So too is a well-functioning legal system that brings greater certainty to human interactions and provides for the peaceful resolution of disputes. Rising levels of greenhouse gases in the atmosphere and growing economic inequality, among other things, compromise and undermine positive freedom by depriving people of choices they would otherwise have to improve their quality of life. More intense coastal flooding and the growing number of droughts and heat waves, for example, limit where people can safely live, make it harder for farmers to make a living, and increase health risks for those without air conditioning.

While freedom, opportunity, and quality of life are often seen as the objectives of sustainable development, others describe the objective in similar but different terms. Some see the objective as human flourishing.[11] One lawyer thus explains the application of sustainable

---

10. "The answer to the question 'Who governs me?' is logically distinct from the question 'How far does government interfere with me?' It is in this difference that the great contrast between the two concepts of negative and positive liberty, in the end, consists." *Id.* at 22.

11. JOHN R. EHRENFELD & ANDREW J. HOFFMAN, FLOURISHING: A FRANK CONVERSATION ABOUT SUSTAINABILITY (2013).

development to the corporate world: "How can we help corporations live into an aspirational goal of creating and encouraging human flourishing?" Somewhat differently, the U.N. General Assembly resolution endorsing the SDGs expressed the objective in terms of human dignity and human rights.[12] "[T]he dignity of the human person is fundamental," it says, pledging that "no one will be left behind."[13] Human dignity can be defined simply as "the inherent equal worth of everyone, everywhere."[14] The use of human rights language to describe the objective of sustainable development also captures the concern for the well-being of each human. In sum, sustainable development at its core is about improving the quality of each human life for present and future generations.

2. Sustainable Development Requires the Practice of Integrated Decision-Making

To improve human quality of life, we need to make better decisions, using a more complete decision-making framework. Integrated decision-making is the key means for achieving the objective of better quality of life for all in present and future generations. As indicated in Chapter 1, it is the central action principle of sustainable development.[15] The Rio Declaration states: "In order to achieve sustainable development, environmental protection shall constitute an integral part of the development process and cannot be considered in isolation from it."[16] Integrated decision-making applies not only to governments and government agencies at the federal, state, and local levels; it also applies to corporations, businesses, and nongovernmental organizations.

Because sustainable development is a framework for making better decisions, it is not just a lofty thought or sentiment about our aspirations

---

12. *See, e.g.*, Transforming Our World, *supra* note 6, ¶ 8 ("We envisage a world of universal respect for human rights and human dignity. . . .").

13. *Id.* ¶ 4.

14. James R. May & Erin Daly, *The UN Sustainable Development Goals and Human Dignity under Law*, *in* International Environmental Law-Making and Diplomacy Review 2019, at 15 (Tuula Honkonen & Seita Romppanen eds., 2020).

15. John C. Dernbach, *Achieving Sustainable Development: The Centrality and Multiple Facets of Integrated Decisionmaking*, 10 Ind. J. Glob. Legal Stud. 247 (2003).

16. *Rio Declaration*, *supra* note 1, Principle 4.

for the environment, equity, or present or future generations. All too often, people simply miss this when they shorten "sustainable development" to "sustainability" and then conclude that the idea is merely to keep the status quo going or "sustain" things somehow.

As its name indicates, the purpose of integrated decision-making is to integrate different aspects of a project or proposal into the same decision-making process. That process should lead to a better decision. All too often, the economic objectives of a project or proposal come first and remain dominant in a decision-making process in which the social, environmental, and even peace and security aspects of a project or proposal are ignored, downplayed, or not fully considered. Even when these other aspects are considered, projects or proposals frequently focus mainly on economic goals without seeking to meaningfully integrate environmental, social, or security goals. In these cases, environmental, social, and security goals are expressed in terms of minimizing damage and not in terms of, say, improving environmental quality or social conditions (e.g., regenerative agriculture). By contrast, the integrated decision-making process should ideally result in decisions that advance all four of these goals (economic, social, environmental, and security). That is, the project or proposal should result in several types of positive outcomes at the same time—thereby furthering progress toward sustainable development. The idea, in short, is to meet two or more needs with one deed.

The two different figures that follow each capture basic truths about sustainable development. Figure 2.1, perhaps the most commonly used of these figures, suggests that the object of sustainable development is to maximize the positive contribution of human activities to the environment, the economy, and society at the same time. Figure 2.1 also makes clear that a great many decisions do not do that. Because many believe this depiction of sustainable development is inadequate, others have emerged.

Figure 2.2 depicts sustainable development as three concentric, rather than overlapping, circles, and is arguably a more accurate depiction of sustainable development. In this figure, the environment is the outer circle because the environment is the foundation for both society and the economy, and because it is, in fact, larger than both. The economy, the inner circle, is nested within society because it depends on both society and the environment and because it is smaller than both, notwithstanding its enormous impact. Unlike Figure 2.1, which

Figure 2.1 Sustainability and Three Overlapping Circles

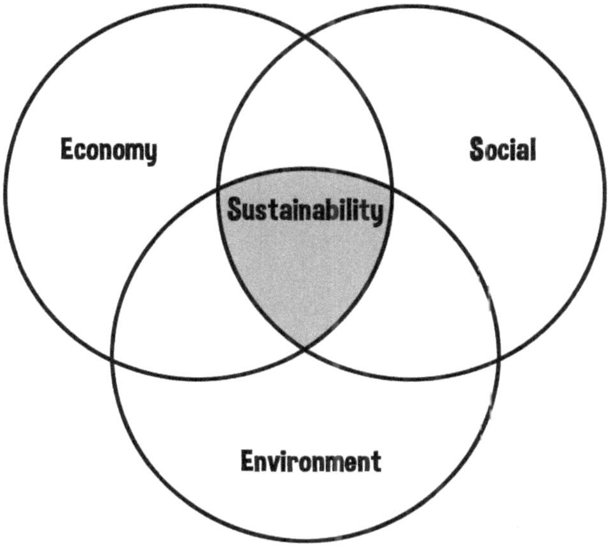

Figure 2.2 Sustainability and Three Concentric Circles

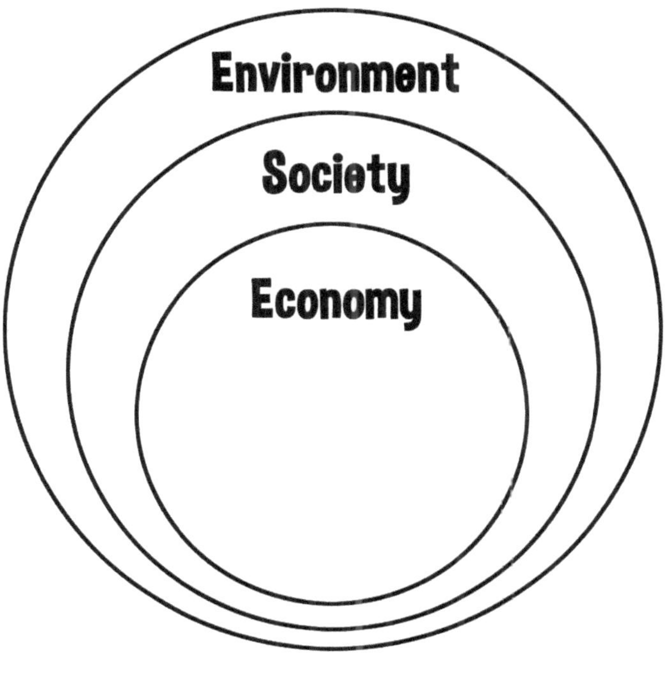

describes a range of decision-making options that include but are not limited to sustainable development, Figure 2.2 is premised on the view that decision making should recognize the centrality of the environment to society, and the centrality of society to the economy.[17]

These two figures each contain basic truths about decision-making for sustainable development. They both show how the environment, the economy, and society are deeply intertwined, and each expresses the relationship in a different way. Neither addresses peace and security, the fourth dimension of sustainable development, although peace and security are foundational to any effort to achieve a sustainable society. As the sustainable development framework is more widely used, we expect that other ways to depict its principles will emerge.

3. Sustainable Development Requires Supportive Governance

Supportive governance serves an essential role in achieving and accelerating the transition to a sustainable society. Governance has both a public component and a private component. Public governance refers to the laws we enact at the local, state, and national governmental levels and also includes agreements between and among countries. These public governance laws are critical to securing a sustainable way of life and include but are not limited to reducing the risks of climate change. We will need much more effective lawmaking at every public governance level to achieve needed progress. For the existential threat of climate change, for example, we will need to enact and modify many public laws to reduce greenhouse gas emissions to net zero or below by 2050.[18]

Public laws are not enough. Actions by private, nonprofit, and for-benefit enterprises are also needed. These private actions, norms, and standards are called private governance. They include certification, auditing, labeling, and reporting programs that can be enforced

---

17. *See, e.g.*, Herman E. Daly & Joshua Farley, Ecological Economics: Principles and Applications 22–24 (2004) (explaining that the economy is contained within the ecosystem, and not the other way around).

18. Legal Pathways to Deep Decarbonization in the United States (Michael B. Gerrard & John C. Dernbach eds., 2019).

through a variety of contractual and transparency-related mechanisms.[19] Many of these private governance standards are expressed under the heading of Environmental, Social, and Governance or ESG. Significantly, the G in ESG stands for corporate governance. Vanderbilt Law School professors Michael Vandenbergh and Jonathan Gilligan point out that it is critical to not simply rely upon the prospect that public governance solutions will finally emerge in time for society to avoid the worst of the climate crisis. Instead, they argue, we need a new complementary approach that draws on "advocacy groups and philanthropists [and] that elicits the participation of corporations, households, and other private sector actors to . . . complement government mitigation efforts. . . ."[20]

Significantly, nearly every major form of public environmental regulation has parallels in private environmental governance.[21] Corporations and other private organizations impose limits on themselves and their suppliers, participate in private associations "or multi-stakeholder groups" that "both set environmental standards for their members and have the power to monitor compliance," or participate in certification programs overseen by nongovernmental organizations.[22] This does not mean that private governance is of equal effectiveness to public governance, but it does mean "that there are more options available to decisionmakers than traditionally believed."[23] Accelerating private governance is no small thing. For example, private corporate greenhouse gas emissions reductions could be as high as one-half billion tons of carbon dioxide equivalent, which is "equal to a regulatory approach that would reduce the emissions of the U.S. transportation sector by a third."[24]

---

19. Michael P. Vandenbergh, *Private Environmental Governance*, 99 Cornell L. Rev. 129 (2013); Errol Meidinger, *Environmental Certification Systems and U.S. Environmental Law: Closer Than You May Think*, 31 ELR 10162 (Feb. 2001).

20. Michael P. Vandenbergh & Jonathan M. Gilligan, Beyond Politics: The Private Governance Response to Climate Change 13 (2017).

21. Sarah E. Light & Eric W. Orts, *Parallels in Public and Private Environmental Governance*, 5 Mich. J. Env't & Admin. L. 1, 12–13 (2015).

22. Vandenbergh & Gilligan, *supra* note 20, at 24–29. They do so in response to pressure from advocacy groups, investors, lenders, employees, and corporate and retail customers, as well as in anticipation of future government regulation. *Id.*

23. *Id.* at 53.

24. *Id.* at 224.

Lawyers are among society's best-equipped professionals to lead the change in our public and private governance laws. Lawyers are already trained to use the legal levers necessary at the international, national, state, and local levels to advocate, draft, and help implement laws that can deliver more sustainable outcomes. Lawyers are also important players in improving private governance because they counsel private actors, who do or don't do certain things related to sustainable development or climate change based in significant part on the advice provided by their lawyers.

Sustainable development also requires changes in personal behavior. Harnessing individual effort and participation is likely to mean that the U.S.'s response to climate change would be more effective, and the speed and size of emissions reductions greater, than it would otherwise be.[25] Activities that are under the "direct, substantial control of the individual and that are not undertaken in the scope of the individual's employment" are responsible for about one-third of U.S. greenhouse gas emissions and 8 percent of global greenhouse gas emissions.[26] Personal behavior changes are not a substitute for changes in public or private governance, and an undue emphasis on personal behavior risks trivializing the effort to reduce greenhouse gas emissions and move toward a more sustainable society. But personal behavior changes can modify social norms dramatically and, as we have seen by the increase of those working at home since the beginning of the COVID-19 pandemic, rapidly.

Personal behavior matters for lawyers because of the many roles that lawyers play in society—roles described more fully in Chapter 3. Law firms and other law offices can serve as models for sustainability by the internal actions they take and the leadership they display with their clients, within their profession, and in their communities. They can do that because of the effort of individuals or teams of individuals in these offices.

The interdependent relationships of public governance, private governance, and personal behaviors are shown in Figure 2.3 in the

---

25. Michael P. Vandenbergh & Ann C. Steinemann, *The Carbon-Neutral Individual*, 82 N.Y.U. L. Rev. 1673, 1739–40 (2007) (efforts directed at individuals could "buy time for new technologies or regulatory measures, create incentives for the development of these measures in the first place, and make them more effective when they are adopted").

26. *Id.* at 1690.

Figure 2.3 The Governance Jellyfish

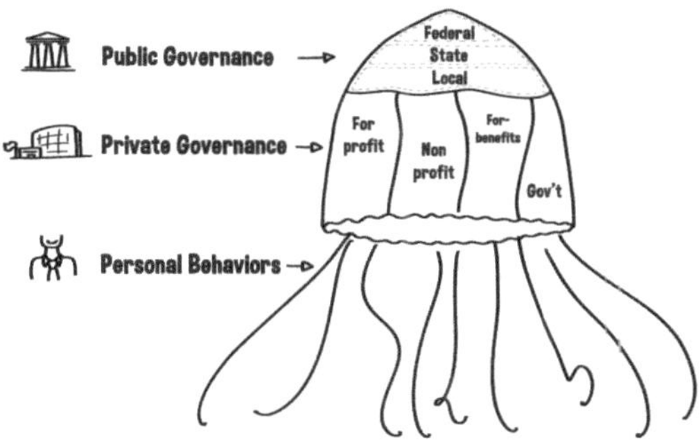

shape of a particular jellyfish species, *Turritopsis dohrnii*. This jellyfish, sometimes called the "immortal jellyfish" because of some of its regenerative properties,[27] is an apt metaphor for our collective work of creating a sustainable society.

Figure 2.4 shows the human sustainable development project in the form of the journey of the jellyfish. In their own ways, the public sector, private sector, and individuals need to contribute to progress on

Figure 2.4 Moving toward a Sustainable Society

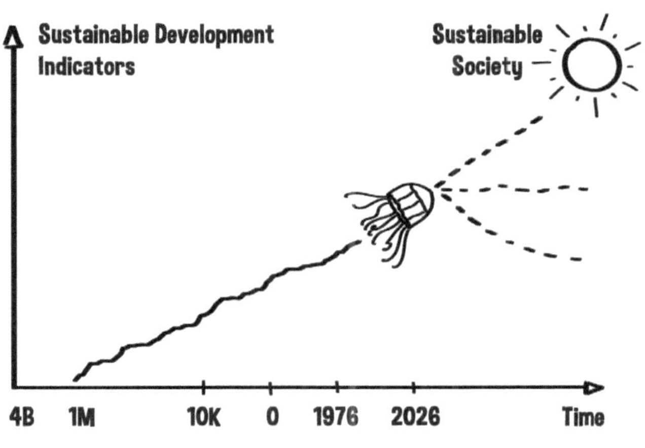

27. Ker Than, *"Immortal" Jellyfish Swarm World's Oceans*, NAT'L GEOGRAPHIC (Jan. 29, 2009), https://www.nationalgeographic.com/animals/article/immortal-jellyfish-swarm-oceans-animals.

the sustainability journey. Personal behavior can affect and be affected by private-sector behavior. Similarly, public actions can influence and be influenced by both private governance and personal behavior. Without each of these three, it is not likely we will get to a sustainable society and get there on time. All parts of the jellyfish need to start working better together to create the kind of self-regenerating capability needed for this and future generations to thrive.

This chapter has described the principles that grow out of the history of sustainable development described in Chapter 1. They provide the foundation for the rest of this book and are highlighted in Figure 2.5, the Difference Maker—Version 1, which will reappear in increasingly complete versions in later chapters as key topics are introduced. This version reflects the four building blocks that form the base of human efforts to build a sustainable society: environmental, social, economic, and security. Also shown are the three primary means for effectuating change toward more sustainable outcomes: public governance, private governance, and personal behaviors.

Figure 2.5 The Difference Maker—Version 1

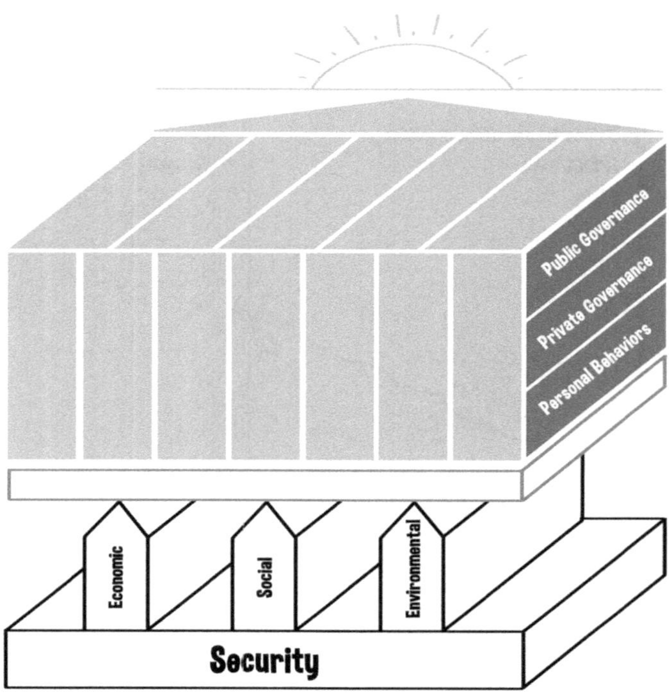

3

Lawyers' Responsibilities to Clients and the Public Good

Now that the history and basic principles of sustainable development are clear, this chapter identifies legal and ethical principles that impose responsibilities on lawyers. It provides guidance for lawyers generally and especially for lawyers working for sustainable development.

As this chapter guides us to see the crucial public role that lawyers play, it also explores why we believe lawyers should foster sustainable development in their professional practice and in their personal lives. This discussion is aimed at helping lawyers identify and understand the requirements applicable to them under our laws and ethics system when applying sustainable development principles to the practice of law. It does not propose new ethical rules.[1] Nor does it describe what the law and rules of conduct *should* be. Rather, it synthesizes the law and existing rules to explain what lawyers can do and—we

1. Some scholars assert the need for specific rules to protect the environment and, thus, sustainable development. *See, e.g.*, J. William Futrell, *Environmental Ethics, Legal Ethics, and Codes of Professional Responsibility*, 27 LOY. L.A. L. REV. 825, 836–39 (1994) (discussing the growth of environmental law and noting the need for new ethical rules); Tom Lininger, *Green Ethics for Lawyers*, 57 B.C. L. REV. 61 (2016).

argue—should do to seek a more just and sustainable society. In exploring these issues, we consider applicable common law, statutory law, and regulatory law, including the American Bar Association's (ABA's) Model Rules of Professional Conduct ("Model Rules" or "Rules").[2]

Rather than limiting consideration to ethical rules of lawyer conduct,[3] this chapter recognizes the larger system of lawyer regulation, which includes the common law (such as contracts, torts, and agency law) and statutory and regulatory law (such as criminal law and requirements set by administrative agencies).[4] Lawyer regulation is broader than the application of the ethics rules alone, which provide the template for state disciplinary authorities. References to the *Restatement of the Law Governing Lawyers* provide insight into this larger system of lawyer regulation and discipline as they include references to malpractice and agency law. Thus, the description of lawyer regulation refers not only to the hard law of statutory mandates but also to the more limited realm of legal ethics and norms that encourage lawyer behavior, such as taking steps to reform the law.

The Constitution's call to "secure the Blessings of Liberty to ourselves and our Posterity"[5]—that is, the founders' pledge to a principle of sustainable development—is itself a normative aspiration for all of us to make the system better for this and future generations. The first sentence of the Preamble to the Model Rules, which identifies lawyer roles, derives its power from this norm: "A lawyer, as a member of the legal profession, is a representative of clients, an officer of the legal system and a public citizen having special responsibility for the quality of justice."[6]

---

2. Like other model or uniform legislation, the Model Rules do not apply to a lawyer unless the lawyer's jurisdiction of licensure adopts the rules. Today all states have adopted the template of the Model Rules, but states have amended aspects of the rules in both minor and significant ways.

3. The chapter does not explore rules relating to conflicts of interest, confidentiality, safekeeping client property, or selling a law practice. While these and other rules are important, they are not used here in the focus on lawyer duties relating to sustainable development.

4. *See, e.g.*, 17 C.F.R. pt. 205 (Standards of Professional Conduct for Attorneys Appearing and Practicing before the [Securities & Exchange] Commission in the Representation of an Issuer).

5. U.S. Const. pmbl.

6. Model Rules of Pro. Conduct, Preamble, para. [1] (Am. Bar Ass'n 2020).

All lawyers need to know the law and ethics rules applicable to them and, to the greatest degree possible, understand what they prohibit, require, and permit. Some lawyers believe that disciplinary boards should sanction lawyers who work for clients who perpetuate the carbon-intensive economy. They see these lawyers as unethical because their clients cause harm or add to the cumulative effects of climate disruption. Other lawyers believe that their ethical duty to clients prevents them from acting to protect society from the climate crisis and other dangers. The relationship between legal ethics and sustainable development resides in the space between these poles. This chapter provides three simple and memorable touchstones to help lawyers understand and fulfill their responsibilities. Each requires a good-faith commitment by lawyers to fulfill their duties to the best of their abilities.

1. Obey and Respect the Law

The first touchstone is compliance with the law. It is the first principle of our democracy and of all governments adhering to the rule of law. The duty to obey (to fully comply with) the law is a given in our legal system, making this touchstone a duty as well as an ethical principle. No person is above the law.[7] Theodore Roosevelt declared this foundational principle emphatically: "No man is above the law and no man is below it: nor do we ask any man's permission when we ask him to obey it."[8] The Nuremberg Trial affirmed this principle of accountability.[9] Indeed, for the legal system to work, all people, including lawyers, must act together to support the public's belief and confidence in the law.[10]

---

7. The principle "Nemo est supra leges" dates to the beginnings of the rule of law.

8. Theodore Roosevelt, Third Annual Message to Congress (later called "the state of the union") (Dec. 7, 1903), https://www.presidency.ucsb.edu/documents/third-annual-message-16.

9. Justice Robert H. Jackson, Closing Arguments for Conviction of Nazi War Criminals (July 26, 1946) (rebutting arguments that orders by superior officers shielded the defendants), https://www.roberthjackson.org/wp-content/uploads/2015/01/Closing_Argument_for_Conviction_of_Nazi_War_Criminals.pdf.

10. *What Is the Rule of Law*, ABA, https://www.americanbar.org/advocacy/rule_of_law/what-is-the-rule-of-law/ (last visited Aug. 1, 2021).

Each person owes legal duties to society, such as the duty to obey the law. These duties are found in both civil and criminal law,[11] Lawyers are subject to the law.[12] Obviously, lawyers are not above the law,[13] and their clients are not above the law either.[14] Their clients are "legal persons," a term that includes both human persons and corporations. "Corporations help structure and facilitate the activities of human beings, to be sure, and their 'personhood' often serves as a useful legal fiction. But they are not themselves members of 'We the People' by whom and for whom our Constitution was established."[15]

The law, including the rules of legal ethics, has evolved as a necessity to maintain the public good under the legal system. Even though the Rules of Professional Conduct do not displace the law, legal ethical rules and norms are essential to maintain and enhance the profession in hopes of securing a sustainable system for this and future generations. The fact that the law treats lawyers differently than other citizens in some cases, does not mean that lawyers have a "free card" against liability.[16] The *Restatement (Third) of the Law Governing Lawyers* notes that generally "a lawyer is subject to liability to a client or nonclient when a nonlawyer would be in similar circumstances."[17] Against this default of general liability, the law provides limited immunity to

11. *See* Irma S. Russell, *The Logic of Legal Remedies and the Relative Weight of Norms: Assessing the Public Interest in the Tort Reform Debate*, 39 Akron L. Rev. 1053 (2006).

12. *See, e.g.*, Model Rules of Pro. Conduct r. 8.4(d) cmt. 2 (stating lawyers are "personally answerable to the entire criminal law," noting difficult tasks of line drawing in determining conduct that should result in lawyers being held "professionally answerable," and including within category of professional misconduct offenses "involving violence, dishonesty, breach of trust, or serious interference with the administration of justice").

13. Restatement (Third) of the Law Governing Lawyers § 1 (Am. L. Inst. 2000).

14. *See* Principles of Corp. Governance § 2.01(b) (Am. L. Inst. 1994) (stating corporation is "obliged, to the same extent as a natural person, to act within the boundaries set by law").

15. Citizens United v. Fed. Election Comm'n, 558 U.S. 310, 466 (2010) (Stevens, J., dissenting).

16. Restatement (Third) of the Law Governing Lawyers § 56 (Am. L. Inst. 2000) (stating general rule that "a lawyer is subject to liability to a client or nonclient when a nonlawyer would be in similar circumstances" and noting exception of § 57 and additions of §§ 48–55).

17. *Id.*

lawyers in well-defined circumstances.[18] For example, the litigation privilege bars a claim for defamation against a lawyer when the statement at issue was made to a person potentially involved in the proceeding as part of the lawyer's role as counsel in the proceeding.[19] The law and rules relating to lawyer conduct impose heightened duties on lawyers for conduct when the conduct could undermine the legal system or mislead clients.[20] For example, the duties of candor and truthfulness stated in the Rules impose higher standards on lawyers than would otherwise apply.[21] The Model Rules prohibit lawyers from stating or implying "an ability to influence improperly a government agency or official or to achieve results by means that violate the rules."[22] The Rules emphasize the duty of lawyers to uphold the legal system and to foster public respect of and confidence in the legal system.[23] Under the Rules, lawyer misconduct includes the failure to "inform the appropriate professional authority" of another lawyer's violation of the Rules of Professional Conduct that "raises a substantial question as to the lawyer's honesty, trustworthiness, or fitness as a lawyer in other respects."[24] Thus, boards and courts may discipline lawyers for a failure to live up to high standards of honesty. Disciplinary authorities may impose sanctions on lawyers for conduct though it arises entirely in the lawyer's personal life rather than in a representation.[25]

Lawyers who are leaders in sustainable development see Touchstone 1 as inadequate by itself, reasoning that the failure of existing

---

18. *Id.* § 57.

19. *See id.*; Restatement (Second) of Torts § 587 (Am. L. Inst. 1977) (recognizing lawyer privilege to publish defamatory communications related to judicial proceeding).

20. *See, e.g.*, Model Rules of Pro. Conduct r. 8.4(d) (engaging in conduct "prejudicial to the administration of justice" is misconduct), r. 8.4(e) (suggesting that the lawyer has the "ability to influence improperly a government agency or official"). *See also id.* r. 3.3 (candor to tribunals), r. 4.1 (truthfulness in statements to others) (Am. Bar Ass'n 2020).

21. *See, e.g.*, *id.* r. 8.3, 8.4, 3.4, 1.2(d), 3.3, 4.1; Restatement (Third) of the Law Governing Lawyers §§ 48–55 (Am. L. Inst. 2000).

22. Model Rules of Pro. Conduct r. 8.3, 8.4, 3.4, 1.2(d), 3.3, 4.1 (Am. Bar Ass'n 2020). Model Rule 8.4 recognizes types of misconduct beyond violations of law.

23. *See, e.g.*, *id.*

24. *Id.* r. 8.3(a).

25. *See, e.g.*, *id.* r. 8.4 and comments (noting personal acts not involving a representation of a client can be sanctionable under the rules).

law to address unreasonable dangers—such as the climate crisis—means lawyers should—as we discuss under Touchstone 2—help clients learn about ways to enhance their benefits and reduce their risks. They advocate advancing sustainable development to provide more beneficial results than required by current law. In addition, as we discuss under Touchstone 3, both the client and the lawyer have the right to advocate for law reform to protect and advance sustainable development.

2. Serve Each Client's Legitimate Interests Competently and within the Bounds of the Law

The second touchstone is the lawyer's duty to advance clients' legitimate interests by lawful means. The U.S. Supreme Court made this point by stating that a lawyer "works for the advancement of justice while faithfully protecting the *rightful* interests of his clients."[26] The Scope section of the Model Rules of Professional Conduct acknowledges that the model presents "rules of reason" that "should be interpreted with reference to the purposes of legal representation and of the law itself."[27] The common law of agency (the law governing a relationship in which one person has legal authority to act for another) and the Model Rules based on agency law limit lawyers to serving only legitimate client interests. The Preamble to the Model Rules states that lawyers have an "obligation zealously to protect and pursue a client's *legitimate* interests, *within the bounds of the law*."[28]

It is axiomatic that to serve client interests, the lawyer must be competent.[29] Lawyers and clients create a "representation" under the common law of contract.[30] The lawyer must serve the client's legitimate

26. Hickman v. Taylor, 329 U.S. 495, 510–11 (1947) (emphasis added).

27. Model Rules of Pro. Conduct, Preamble & Scope, para. [14] (Am. Bar Ass'n 2020). For example, Model Rule 1.6(b)(5) states the duty of lawyers to reveal information to comply with law or a court. The duty exists by virtue of the law or court order rather than by virtue of the ethics rule. Similarly, comment 5 states that lawyers "should use the law's procedures only for legitimate purposes." *See* Model Rules of Pro. Conduct, Preamble & Scope, para. [5] (Am. Bar Ass'n 2020).

28. *Id.*, Preamble, para. [9] (2006) (emphasis added).

29. *Id.* r. 1.1.

30. *Id.*, Preamble, para. [17] (2020) (stating that "principles of substantive law external to these Rules determine whether a client-lawyer relationship exists").

interests within this representation competently and diligently.[31] A lawyer's duties are also based on common-law principles of agency law and include the duty of loyalty.[32] The Model Rules contextualize the law of agency to the specific relationship of lawyers and clients and emphasize duties to the system of justice as well as those of an agent to a principal.[33] Based on these durable principles, clients should have confidence that their lawyer has the education and preparation necessary to serve their legitimate interests and that the lawyer will act with competence and diligence to advance their legitimate objectives without violating the law.[34] When a lawyer violates the law, she may also violate the Model Rules by the same conduct and face penalties under both the legal system and the disciplinary system.[35]

Lawyers have a duty to explain the law rather than simply stating the black letter law or telling the client what the client wants to hear. The Model Rules emphasize that a lawyer's job is to serve as a reliable advisor, rather than simply making the best argument to justify client actions.[36] Model Rule 1.2(d) prohibits advising or assisting a client when the lawyer knows the client's conduct will be criminal or fraudulent. The lawyer's knowledge regarding this issue can be inferred from circumstances. In a formal opinion in April 2020, the ABA clarified the standard to emphasize that intentional blindness to or conscious avoidance of facts is not a shield against Rule 1.2(d).[37] The opinion also noted that in some circumstances other rules require lawyers to

---

31. *Id.* r. 1.1, 1.3.

32. "Agency encompasses a wide and diverse range of relationships and circumstances. The elements of common-law agency are present in the relationships between employer and employee, corporation and officer, client and lawyer, and partnership and general partner." RESTATEMENT (THIRD) OF AGENCY § 1.01 (AM. L. INST. 2006).

33. *See, e.g.*, Cmty. for Creative Non-Violence v. Reid, 490 U.S. 730, 740 (1989).

34. *See, e.g.*, MODEL RULES OF PRO. CONDUCT r. 1.2(d) (AM. BAR ASS'N 2020) (stating lawyer's duty not to counsel a client to engage, or assist a client, in conduct that the lawyer knows is criminal or fraudulent).

35. *See In re* Fisher, 202 P.3d 1196 (Colo. 2009) (rejecting argument that double jeopardy clause of U.S. constitution applies to discipline). *See also* Douglas R. Richmond, *Dishonest or Unworthy Clients: Pink Flags*, ABA (2019), https://www.americanbar.org/groups/professional_responsibility/dishonest-or-unworthy-clients--pink-flags/.

36. MODEL RULES OF PRO. CONDUCT r. 1.2, 2.1 (AM. BAR ASS'N 2020).

37. ABA Comm. on Ethics & Pro. Resp., Formal Op. 491, Obligations under Rule 1.2(d) to Avoid Counseling or Assisting in a Crime or Fraud in Non-Litigation Settings (2020), https://www.americanbar.org/content/dam/aba/administrative/professional_responsibility/aba-formal-opinion-491.pdf.

"inquire further in order to help the client avoid crime or fraud, to avoid professional misconduct, and to advance the client's legitimate interest."[38]

In the context of sustainable development, a particularly important part of this second touchstone is the lawyer's duty as an advisor. Loyalty to the principal is the core of agency law and all agents, including lawyers, corporate officers, and other fiduciaries, owe the principal loyal service.[39] The lawyer's general duty of loyalty to the client is well established.[40] Thus, the traditional role of the lawyer as an advisor is broader than simply advising on the state of the law or legal consequences.[41] In addition to mandating that the lawyer "exercise independent professional judgment and render candid advice,"[42] Model Rule 2.1 emphasizes a broad approach to the lawyer's role as an advisor. The first comment to the rule emphasizes that the lawyer "should not be deterred from giving candid advice by the prospect that the advice will be unpalatable to the client."[43] The second comment indicates that advice "couched in narrow legal terms may be of little value to a client, especially where practical considerations, such as cost or effects on other people, are predominant."[44] The rule also makes clear that lawyers may include in their advice "considerations such as moral, economic, social and political factors that may be relevant to the client's situation."[45]

Moral, economic, social, and political factors are implicated in nearly all sustainable development issues. Under Model Rule 2.1 and

38. *Id.* The Comments to Model Rule 1.2(d) provide guidance on how a lawyer should interpret Rule 1.2(d), explaining that when the lawyer learns that a client intends to commit a crime or engage in fraud, the lawyer must explain the limits on the lawyer's role and withdraw from the representation if the client continues to pursue wrongful conduct. *See also* Model Rules of Pro. Conduct r. 1.16(b)(2).

39. The duty of loyalty is a core value of all agents and fiduciaries. This includes directors and officers of corporations. "Corporate officers and directors are not permitted to use their position of trust and confidence to further their private interest." Guth v. Loft, 5 A.2d 503, 510 (Del. 1939).

40. *See, e.g.*, Restatement (Third) of the Law Governing Lawyers § 16 cmt. b (Am. L. Inst. 2000) (giving underlying rationale of lawyer duties as a fiduciary and noting that "the lawyer's competence, diligence, and loyalty are therefore vital").

41. Model Rules of Pro. Conduct r. 2.1 cmts. 2, 3 (Am. Bar Ass'n 2020).

42. *Id.* r. 2.1.

43. *Id.* cmt. 1.

44. *Id.* cmt. 2.

45. *Id.* r. 2.1.

the lawyer's general duty of loyalty to the client, a lawyer who sees risks or opportunities for her client related to climate change or sustainable development has a duty to educate her clients about these risks or opportunities. Such advice may also be appropriate "when a lawyer knows that a client proposes a course of action that is likely to result in substantial adverse legal consequences to the client."[46] As noted earlier, the Model Rules explicitly permit this kind of advice whether the client wants to hear it or not.[47] As the effects of climate change grow to further inhibit sustainable development and legislatures pass new legal mandates, such advice will be increasingly important.

This approach applies not only to individuals who are clients; it also applies to corporate clients. Lawyers have special opportunities to advise corporate clients about both their obligations under the law and the opportunities for furthering sustainable development. Statutes permit the organization of corporations only for lawful purposes.[48] Likewise, legal persons such as corporations are subject to the same duties as natural persons. A corporation "[i]s obliged, to the same extent as a natural person, to act within the boundaries set by law."[49] While lawyers and judges sometimes assume that corporations must maximize shareholder profit in every decision, this view is called into question by the foundational laws authorizing the formation of corporate entities and recognition that corporations may further public purposes.[50] In advising corporations under Model Rule 2.1, lawyers should not only remind these clients that they are obliged to comply with law. They can and should also advise their corporate clients that they "may take into account ethical considerations that are reasonably regarded as appropriate to the responsible conduct of business" and may "devote a reasonable amount of resources to public welfare, humanitarian,

---

46. *Id.* cmt. 5.

47. *Id.* cmt. 1 (noting the lawyer "should not be deterred from giving candid advice by the prospect that the advice will be unpalatable to the client").

48. *See, e.g.*, DEL. CODE ANN. tit. 8, § 101(b) (1953) (stating corporation "may be incorporated or organized under this chapter to conduct or promote any lawful business or purposes, except as may otherwise be provided by the Constitution or other law of this State").

49. PRINCIPLES OF CORP. GOVERNANCE § 2.01 (AM. LAW. INST. 1994). In other words, the corporate form of doing business does not provide immunity from laws.

50. *See, e.g.*, LYNN STOUT, THE SHAREHOLDER VALUE MYTH: HOW PUTTING SHAREHOLDERS FIRST HARMS INVESTORS, CORPORATIONS, AND THE PUBLIC (2012).

educational, and philanthropic purposes."[51] In that way, lawyers can encourage their clients to advance sustainable development.

Lawyers also have ethical duties regarding truthfulness that are relevant in this context. Model Rule 4.1 prohibits lawyers from knowingly making "a false statement of material fact or law to a third person." It also generally prohibits a lawyer from failing to disclose a material fact to a third person "when disclosure is necessary to avoid assisting a criminal or fraudulent act by a client" except when the rule on confidentiality prohibits that disclosure.[52] Potential liability under common law fraud also incentivizes truthful communications by lawyers as well as clients.[53] Model Rule 3.3 emphasizes the duty of truthfulness to tribunals.[54] Although the rules do not expressly state the lawyer's duty of truthfulness to *clients*, the general duty of loyalty to the client and the overarching requirement that lawyers act in the best interests of the client make truthfulness a core ingredient of the lawyer's communications with clients.[55]

These duties have significant consequences for an attorney's approach to many sustainable development issues. For example, the abundance of misinformation about climate change in the public domain and the growing body of science in this area make the lawyer's role in providing accurate information of paramount importance. Lawyers may be able to provide valuable advice by predicting changes in the regulatory and legal landscape and the likelihood that client interests may change in the future. Both the general duty of loyalty and the mandate of Model Rule 2.1 mean that attorneys should discuss with clients ways the clients' interests may be affected by foreseeable changes in circumstances such as extreme weather and other effects of

---

51. PRINCIPLES OF CORP. GOVERNANCE § 2.01 (AM. LAW INST. 1994).

52. MODEL RULES OF PRO. CONDUCT r. 4.1 (AM. BAR ASS'N 2020).

53. RESTATEMENT (THIRD) OF THE LAW GOVERNING LAWYERS § 56 (AM. L. INST. 2000) (stating general rule that "a lawyer is subject to liability to a client or nonclient when a nonlawyer would be in similar circumstances" and noting exception of § 57 and additions of §§ 48–55).

54. MODEL RULES OF PRO. CONDUCT r. 3.3 (AM. BAR ASS'N 2020).

55. *See id.* r. 1.4 (communication with the client); *see generally* Raymond J. McKoski, *The Truth Be Told: The Need for a Model Rule Defining a Lawyer's Duty of Candor to a Client*, 99 IOWA L. REV. BULL. 73 (2014).

the carbon economy. Thus, the ABA recommends that lawyers advise "clients of the risks and opportunities that climate change provides."[56]

Future legal changes also are sometimes foreseeable. This means lawyers should incorporate these changes into their advice to clients. For example, before adoption of the Comprehensive Environmental Response, Compensation, and Liability Act of 1980 (CERCLA),[57] companies often disposed of hazardous substances by unregulated dumping. While disposal was not generally against the law, the dangers to human health and the environment ultimately led Congress to pass CERCLA, imposing retroactive liability to finance the cleanup of hazardous sites.[58] Lawyers who advised clients not to dump hazardous substances before CERCLA were not only smart; they were also fulfilling their duty to advise of the foreseeable event that Congress would pass a law to require that polluters pay for the harm done by even historic disposal. The widespread nature of the problem was known to the legal community and the general public. Legislation relating to greenhouse gas emissions is arguably as necessary today as CERCLA was to address the hazardous substance disposal problem in 1980. The question is not whether the lawyer believes that such legislation is needed or appropriate; the question is more objective—whether the possibility of enactment of such legislation is foreseeable, and if such legislation is enacted, whether it is likely to impact the client's legitimate interests.

3. Advance Justice, Law Reform, and the Public Interest

This touchstone calls on lawyers to play an important role in building our legal system and ethics rules to help produce a sustainable society. Touchstone 3 provides opportunities to serve society through practical wisdom.[59] The lawyer's role as a "public citizen" with "special

---

56. Am. Bar Ass'n House of Delegates, Res. 111 (2019), https://www.americanbar.org/content/dam/aba/directories/policy/annual-2019/111-annual-2019.pdf.

57. U.S.C. §§ 9601–75.

58. *See* Chevron Mining Inc. v. United States, No. 15-2209, 2017 WL 3045887 (10th Cir. July 19, 2017).

59. The Model Rules deal with and seek to inspire this role in the rules relating to public service. *See, e.g.*, Model Rules of Pro. Conduct r. 6.1–6.5 (Am. Bar Ass'n 2020).

responsibility for the quality of justice"[60] is at the heart of law reform when laws fail to protect people fully. As outlined in Chapter 1, sustainable development is a normative decision-making framework and not yet a full body of law. Nevertheless, it is foreseeable that it will be more fully incorporated into law. "As a public citizen, a lawyer should seek improvement of the law, access to the legal system, the administration of justice and the quality of service rendered by the legal profession."[61] Law reform is the mechanism for developing laws to combat inequality and to address emerging risks to people and society.[62] The Model Rules do not require lawyers to change the law but do urge lawyers to play an important role in law reform. The responsibility of lawyers as public citizens is broad, covering the full range of actions that serve society. These include community service and pro bono representations, serving in public office, supporting governmental and community initiatives that benefit the public, improving our system of justice, and reforming the law. Lawyers are an important resource for law reform because they have the training, skills, and influence to help clients see nonapparent benefits in the changing legal landscape and to further common-law and statutory protections.[63] The Preamble to the Model Rules articulates the lawyer's duty to strive to improve the law and the legal profession and to exemplify the legal profession's ideals of public service.[64] This responsibility also implicates the duty of competence. The Preamble states that "a lawyer should cultivate knowledge of the law beyond its use for clients" and "employ that knowledge in reform of the law,"[65] suggesting that competence in the law requires more than expertise in your practice area or a statutory regime. As we said in the introduction, lawyers have advocated for, drafted, and defended a wide variety of major laws over the course of U.S. history,

60. *Id.*, Preamble, para. [1].

61. *Id.* para. [6].

62. For example, before Justice Thurgood Marshall became a justice on the Supreme Court, he advanced civil rights for African Americans and other minorities through challenging discriminatory laws. Similarly, before Justice Ruth Bader Ginsberg was appointed to the Court, she brought constitutional claims to correct gender-based discrimination.

63. *See* Am. Bar Ass'n House of Delegates Res. 111 (2019), https://www.americanbar.org/content/dam/aba/directories/policy/annual-2019/111-annual-2019.pdf.

64. Model Rules of Pro. Conduct, Preamble, para. [7] (Am. Bar Ass'n 2020).

65. *Id.* para. [6] (parsing the duty to "seek improvement of the law" as an attribute of the lawyer as public citizen and to "reform of the law" as part of her duty as a "member of a learned profession").

including the canon of environmental laws to protect people and the environment. The lawyers who worked to draft and pass these laws give us examples of lawyers as public citizens.

A new wave of lawyers is now seeking to address climate disruption and other threats to public well-being. While ethics rules do not mandate a level of effort to change the law and do not provide sanctions against lawyers for failing to embrace a leadership role, they acknowledge the legitimacy of this role and the lawyer's role in improving the law. Thus, our ethics norms provide encouragement for lawyers to be leaders for legal reform.[66] Indeed, we conclude this book, in Chapter 11, by urging you to help reform the law to achieve a more sustainable society. Without leaders who advocate for improved laws, it is highly unlikely that we will have a sustainable society for ourselves and future generations.

Lawyers who follow the three touchstones identified here will serve their clients, the legal system, and society, and they will advance sustainable development. Following the first two touchstones helps lawyers stay out of trouble. Fulfilling the third touchstone offers opportunities for lawyers—perhaps as never before—to help shape a safer and fairer economy and country. The role lawyers historically have played in law reform, their skills in logic and persuasion, and the special place they occupy as public citizens all mean that lawyers can and should help society take the actions needed now to address multiple threats to our future, including climate change. These touchstones also provide a path toward personal fulfillment for lawyers who commit themselves to serving their clients and society and to fostering sustainable development.

They also provide the foundation for a lawyer's work toward this end, as Figure 3.1 shows. This version of the Difference Maker figure shows the three ethical touchstones. The next versions will depict legal work and leadership to make a difference.

---

66. *See* Tom Lininger, *No Privilege to Pollute: Expanding the Crime-Fraud Exception to the Attorney-Client Privilege*, 105 Minn. L. Rev. 113, 140 (2020) (arguing that lawyer assistance in connection with a knowing emission of a pollutant should be admissible as evidence in court and not shielded under attorney-client privilege because the privilege facilitates violations of environmental regulations).

Figure 3.1 Difference Maker Version 2

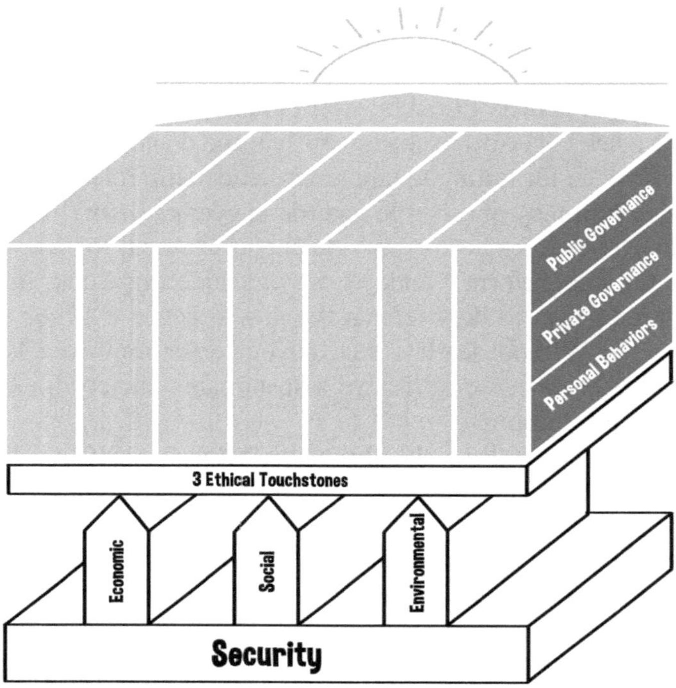

While doctors take the Hippocratic oath, promising to "do no harm," the Model Rules ask more. They charge lawyers with the duty to serve clients within the law; to serve the legal system; and, as public citizens, to embrace their "special responsibility for the quality of justice."[67] While the Rules do not define the lawyer's role of "public citizen," the general meaning of serving society is clear enough. Lawyers are central to the effort to build a sustainable society, and the law and ethical rules provide a solid basis for this work.

67. MODEL RULES OF PRO. CONDUCT, Preamble, para. [1] (AM. BAR ASS'N 2020).

4

How Lawyers Use Sustainable Development in Law Practice

This chapter shows how a growing number of lawyers are already applying sustainable development in law practice. In so doing, it highlights the kinds of questions that lawyers are asking about specific projects, proposals, and issues that clients bring them. This chapter then shows that this decision-making framework is being employed in nearly every field of law and by lawyers using a wide variety of legal skills.

1. Lawyers Are Using the Sustainable Development Decision-Making Framework

Many lawyers use a sustainable development framework to help generate better and more sustainable decisions, whether required by specific laws or not. The framework has two basic elements: process and results.

a. Process: They Urge Their Clients to Consider a Legal Issue's Environmental, Social, Economic, and (When Relevant) Peace and Security Aspects

Considering a legal issue's environmental, social, economic, and (when relevant) peace and security aspects is the first step in integrated decision-making for sustainable development. Many of these questions are addressed as part of the review for proposed major federal actions that significantly affect the quality of the human environment under the National Environmental Policy Act (NEPA).[1] Except where a similar analysis is already required by NEPA or another law, sustainable development enlarges the scope of the traditional decision-making process. Notwithstanding the broad international definition of development, the economic dimensions of a project or proposal have traditionally received primary attention, while its social and environmental consequences get much less attention. For significant projects, issues, or decisions, then, lawyers who apply the sustainable development framework strive to make sure that all of the major impacts or consequences are identified:

Economic. What are the potential economic impacts (e.g., income, profits) for both the project proponent and the people in the community who will be affected by the project? The potential economic consequences for those other than the project proponent deserve serious consideration.

Social. What are the potential social impacts (e.g., job creation, community, public health and safety, equity, improved governance, human rights)?

Environmental. What are the potential environmental impacts on humans, other species, and the ecosystem (e.g., pollution, waste, greenhouse gas emissions, biodiversity loss)?

Security. What are the potential security impacts of a proposal? For a great many proposals or projects there will be no significant security impacts. But when there are, they deserve serious consideration. A proposed new or enlarged naval base, for example, could be threatened by sea level rise from climate change. Proposals involving significant greenhouse gas emissions could also have significant security implications.

1. 42 U.S.C. § 4332(2)(c).

At this stage, the task is simply to identify potential impacts in a kind of brainstorming exercise. Lawyers might come up with their own list or do so in consultation with the client or technical experts working for the client. The types of impacts considered under NEPA may provide a starting point. Lawyers especially consider impacts that have come up in similar projects or proposals. Some of these impacts are much more important than others. Some impacts are greater or are more likely to occur, for example, or present a significant risk of costly and time-consuming litigation or neighborhood opposition. Some may be of particular importance to the client.

The larger the scale and the greater the impact of the proposal, the more these various dimensions tend to be explored. Similarly, the larger and greater the scale of the impact of the proposal, the more valuable it is to have a process for gathering input from all parts of the affected community.

Lawyers who incorporate the sustainable development framework into their practice characterize significant impacts as opportunities or risks—to the client, the community, and the environment. As a practical matter, proposals or projects with larger adverse impacts are more likely to present greater risks of litigation and adverse litigation outcomes.

Lawyers first help clients identify and assess the significance of the likely opportunities or benefits of the proposal and whether they are environmental, economic, and/or social. Once these are understood, lawyers can explore whether the project can feasibly be designed to create more or different opportunities or benefits.

For significant potential risks or negative impacts, they ask questions like these:

- Are there ways of avoiding or minimizing these risks?
- Are there less damaging ways of achieving the purpose of this proposal?
- Are there less damaging or more beneficial alternatives to this proposal?
- Are there ways to design this proposal to turn risks or negative impacts into positive impacts?

These questions, and dozens like them that can be posed in a myriad of contexts lawyers face, reframe the relationship between economic development and everything else we care about. Instead of assuming that economic development and environmental protection are inherently opposing forces, these questions help people think about ways of designing proposals and making decisions that make these aspects mutually reinforcing. This approach draws on legal skills—for creating the strongest arguments that can responsibly be made for a proposal, anticipating counterarguments, and modifying the proposal to minimize the risk of effective counterarguments.

In the corporate Environmental, Social, and Governance setting, the use of independent metrics to measure each of the three types of impacts described earlier (excluding security) is described in terms of a "triple bottom line," as Chapter 1 notes. The social, economic, and environmental goals are often referred to as "people, profit, and planet." One lawyer captures the definition this way: "The simultaneous pursuit of economic prosperity, environmental stewardship, and social responsibility."

The triple bottom line is an attractive process frame for many lawyers. An attorney who works with business and investors says:

> I see that sustainability is critical to long-term success in business and investment. If you manage your environmental, social, and governance issues and impacts well, you will be more successful in business and investment. There is a lot of data showing that sustainable companies outperform sustainability laggards in their industry significantly and that investment strategies that incorporate environmental, social, and governance metrics tend to do better. Sustainable investment beats unsustainable investment. There are megatrends in terms of social license and laws pushing sustainability (at least in the European Union), as well as transparency and disclosure and competitive pressure for companies to be sustainable. Sustainability is starting to win, but it is not because of law. It is more about economics.

Learning to see in multiple dimensions is not always easy. We tend to see what we know and fail to see what we don't know. Environmental and energy lawyers will see environmental and energy issues that others may miss, and human rights lawyers may see still other issues. For some projects or proposals, many adverse environmental and social effects are obvious, at least to some people. But this is not true for all projects or proposals. It is impossible to integrate additional aspects of a problem into decision-making if one does not even see them. As one attorney explains, sustainable development "requires more holistic thinking than the limits in my air permit. The sustainability frame is good for options, alternatives, and advocacy."

The social dimension of an issue or proposal should be considered of equal importance to its environmental and economic dimensions. Environmental damage that compromises human well-being is almost always unjust. Because sustainable development does not, by principle, adversely affect the environment or people who depend upon the environment, it follows that sustainable development is a way of fostering environmental and social justice as well as protecting human rights. Indeed, many attorneys emphasize the social dimension of sustainable development in their law practice. They pay particular care to the impact that many proposed or ongoing activities have, not only on the environment, but also on people in nearby communities or people who depend for their water, food, or well-being on having a high-quality environment. The environmental justice movement grew out of recognition that many projects and activities disproportionately affect people who are "poor, working class or [in] a community of color."[2] The environmental justice movement now includes lawyers who advocate for basic human rights on behalf of those who may be injured, or who have already been injured, by climate change and other environmentally damaging activities in the United States and around the world.

b. Results: They Urge Their Clients to Achieve Positive Environmental, Social, Economic, and (When Relevant) Peace and Security Outcomes to the Greatest Extent Possible

It is not enough to consider the social, environmental, economic, and security aspects of a proposal. After all, it is possible to consider a significant problem that will occur if a particular decision is made and then do nothing about it. Decision-makers should also achieve significant and measurable progress in environmental protection, social development, and economic development. This is the real effect of

2. Oliver Milman, *Interview, Robert Bullard: "Environmental Justice Isn't Just Slang, It's Real,"* The Guardian (Dec. 20, 2018), https://www.theguardian.com/commentisfree/2018/dec/20/robert-bullard-interview-environmental-justice-civil-rights-movement#:~:text=Robert%20Bullard%20is%20known,environmental%20racism%20in%20the%201980s.

"triple bottom line" thinking. When security is involved, there is a "quadruple bottom line."

Thus, lawyers who employ the sustainable development framework ask questions like the following for every significant decision:

Economic. Will the decision lead to economic opportunities or benefits for the client, the community, and other stakeholders? Have avoidable economic risks to people in the community been eliminated? Are unavoidable risks minimized as much as possible? Will the decision help to ameliorate unjust economic disparities? Will the near-term economic benefits be eliminated by long-term cleanup or disposal costs?

Social. Will the decision lead to social benefits or opportunities? Have avoidable social risks been eliminated? Are unavoidable risks minimized as much as possible? Will the decision help to ameliorate unjust social disparities?

Environmental. Will the decision lead to environmental benefits? Have avoidable environmental risks been eliminated? Are unavoidable risks minimized as much as possible? Will the decision help regenerate important aspects of the environment?

Security (when relevant). Will the decision lead to security benefits? Have avoidable security risks been eliminated? Are unavoidable risks minimized as much as possible?

A critical question is whether any given project or activity should be directed at reducing adverse environmental and social risks or instead be directed at creating environmental and social benefits (along with presumed economic benefits). Because of growing population, resource and energy consumption, and economic development and the substantial cumulative effects of numerous negative impacts over generations, achieving sustainable development requires that we move toward the latter. For a long time, proposals or projects have been justified by saying that they will have significant economic benefits and that their environmental and social costs are less bad than they would otherwise be. If we are to truly make progress toward a sustainable society, we must be able to make positive claims honestly and accurately about all impacts of a decision.

The Sustainable Development Goals (SDGs) are an important guide in furthering sustainable development because they define the overall goals toward which we should be heading. Thus, in thinking about the objectives of a particular project or proposal, many lawyers look at the relevant SDGs and targets and urge their clients to make sure that the project or proposal furthers or will help achieve them. For example, a housing development proposal could be designed to include quality low-income housing, thus aligning with the SDG target of "access for all to adequate, safe and affordable housing and basic services."

2. Lawyers Use the Sustainable Development Framework in Every Field of Law

The primary subject matter of sustainable development law practice varies considerably. It includes climate change and clean energy law, environmental law, corporate law, land use and development law, sustainable infrastructure finance, corporate social responsibility, and human rights. Indeed, no area of law practice is unaffected by climate change and sustainable development.

John Kerry, U.S. special presidential envoy for climate, told the General Assembly of the American Bar Association's 2021 annual meeting that "you are all climate lawyers now, whether you want to be or not." He then described the wide variety of legal work that climate change entails:

> We will need lawyers to aid those displaced by climate fueled storms, and nonprofit lawyers to assist individuals and communities after devastating fires. There'll be local attorneys working tirelessly to recover the soaring cost of adaptation and disaster recovery that would empty public coffers. There are the bankruptcy lawyers assessing the infrastructure risks to their clients and advising on safer, wiser planning. Lawyers will be crucial to all aspects of the multiple transactions necessary to expedite the energy transition and innovative strategies for deep decarbonization ahead of us. There'll be questions of financing and construction contracting, land use, procurement. Some of you will write the laws that will drive these transformative interventions, others of you will administer and enforce them, and some of you may negotiate the international arrangements that helped the world address the climate crisis in all its manifestations.[3]

3. John Kerry, U.S. Presidential Envoy for Climate, Keynote Address to American Bar Association General Assembly Annual Meeting (Aug. 5, 2021), https://lpdd.org/wp-content/uploads/2021/08/John-Kerry-Keynote-Speech-2021-ABA-Hybrid-Annual-Meeting.pdf.

Many lawyers now see issues through a sustainable development lens. Taken together, these lawyers have a broad range of clients, including municipal governments, financial institutions, investors, utilities, industry, state and local governments, property owners, and nongovernmental organizations. As one explains: "I do not have a sustainability practice. I have a sustainability prism that informs, or through which I view, my cases and how my cases should be managed, litigated, or pursued."

Within environmental law, the subject matter of these lawyers' work is also varied. Many do the full range of environmental law work, including air and water pollution, wetlands, endangered species, and waste. Others are more specialized. Some focus on the environmental aspects of transactions and on brownfields redevelopment. Some work in the industrial chemical and agricultural chemical area, representing chemical producers, formulators, and end users of these chemicals. One lawyer, working for a regulatory agency, is helping to "identify strategies that can be used to strengthen compliance other than the traditional inspection and enforcement route."

Some lawyers work primarily or exclusively on climate change, renewable energy, and energy efficiency. They work in a wide variety of private practice, governmental, business, academic, and nongovernmental settings.

Other lawyers are anchored in corporate law, but again, their work involves using a sustainability lens. One corporate lawyer describes his clients as "renewable energy, energy storage, energy efficiency companies, and companies with strong sustainability platforms, products, or services." Others have clients that are social enterprises and impact investors. Several do work for startup companies that want to focus on sustainability, including green technology companies.

Many work primarily in land use and development law. The clients for that work can be buyers or sellers, as well as tenants or lenders. One attorney's client base includes not only developers but also green building and resilient design organizations, eco districts, and companies that are trying to bring "energy efficiency, green energy, and social equity projects into the marketplace." Another has a long-standing client base comprised of "property owners, whether that is hotels, shopping centers, office buildings, apartments, or industrial buildings." The lawyer says: "We were able to take that client base and put solar panels on their roofs and encourage them to enter the green sustainability movement and say, this is good for your business."

Some of these lawyers focus on sustainable infrastructure finance. One does legal work for "development and financing of projects that are mostly for sustainable infrastructure of one kind or another, including renewable energy, energy efficiency, micro grids, water, and wastewater."

Others are engaged in various aspects of social sustainability, including corporate social responsibility and human rights. One attorney explains: "We don't do a lot of environmentally oriented work. Our practice is primarily in the human rights space." The attorney adds that the client base for this kind of work tends to involve multinational corporations operating in developing countries where they or their suppliers incur risks of violating human rights. This client base has expanded over time:

> When I started, our client base was primarily, but not exclusively, oil, gas, and mining companies, who were worried about tort cases and were worried about litigation based on acts of security guards at their facilities. Our practice has grown. We have seen diversification of the client base, including now big banks, apparel companies, private equity firms that are looking at potential investments, and technology companies.

The sustainable development framework also can be employed by nonpracticing attorneys. Some work for nongovernmental organizations that are devoted to addressing climate change and sustainable development. Others are engaged in consulting or run their own businesses.

Sustainable development is not a particular subject matter. It is a perspective or lens that practicing attorneys and nonpracticing attorneys can employ in any legal field.

3. Lawyers Use the Sustainable Development Framework in Nearly Every Type of Legal Work

Whatever their legal skills, lawyers apply them to sustainable development legal work. Nearly any type of skill provides opportunities for doing this work.

a. Client Counseling

Perhaps the most common type of legal work in this context is client counseling, which we discussed in Chapter 3. Much legal work, of course, is traditional client counseling about compliance with statutes, regulations, and other legal requirements, including assistance in complying with those requirements. Other counseling is related to litigation or potential litigation, including enforcement actions. For some lawyers, counseling does not just occur in an office setting. Lawyers who work for corporations may speak to corporate boards of directors about Securities and Exchange Commission reporting and disclosure requirements related to sustainability as well as a whole host of internal and external stakeholders. Lawyers who work for local governments may speak to city councils or zoning boards about a green building project or the use of solar energy in public housing.

In addition to traditional counseling about compliance with applicable laws, lawyers who do sustainability-related work also counsel clients on how to move toward or achieve sustainability. Many lawyers explain, for example, the desirability of options based on reduced cost, greater efficiency, improved reputation, and enhanced likelihood of compliance.

b. Transactions

Sustainable development work in law practice also involves a great deal of transactional work. Brownfields redevelopment—the cleanup of contaminated sites so they can be reused for beneficial purposes—is a good example of this type of work. As one lawyer explains:

> With transactional work, I assist with negotiating the contractual provisions that allocate environmental liability and risk between the parties to a deal. The clients for that work can be buyers or sellers as well as tenants or lenders. With brownfields redevelopment work, I assist in putting together teams to execute remediation strategies for a site. In that role, I serve as an environmental oncologist, excising the environmental cancer impacting a site so redevelopment can occur. The clients for that work are typically developers. In both roles, the ultimate goal is to make sure properties are positioned so they are marketable, lendable, and developable.

There are many other types of transactional work. Some transactional work involves solar energy, including negotiation of power purchase agreements, site agreements, construction agreements, finance agreements, and tax-related counseling. For green leasing, there are transactional issues about setting up a structure such that the owner can get certification under the U.S. Green Building Council's Leadership in Energy and Environmental Design program. For other lawyers, transactional work in an environmental setting involves mergers and acquisitions; private equity deals; and "all sorts of offerings on the public market, including both issuers and underwriters, and strategic litigation counseling." One attorney negotiates contracts between smaller startup companies with a sustainability orientation "and larger companies who are interested in them and their line of business. An example is a set of agreements between a ride-sharing company and major airlines that have an interest in that capability."

c. Litigation

While litigation is a traditional part of legal practice, some lawyers find ways to use it to advance sustainability. A lawyer who does enforcement defense work sees it in a sustainable development context:

> The first step in achieving a resolution with government enforcement is correcting the violation. But compliance programs have sustainability components. Almost always, the system does not work because of sustainability concerns, such as inappropriate consumption of resources or discharge of pollutants. When you fix a system, you fix a process. A lot of sustainability is avoidance—pollution prevention, material substitution, upfront design issues. On a wastewater treatment plan with compliance issues, for example, we are counseling the client to reevaluate the design to incorporate energy sustainability (energy recovery to provide heat and reduce energy usage costs), which can avoid multiple problems, such as noncompliance, permitting, and operational costs.

In many jurisdictions, regulators and prosecutors are amenable to supplemental environmental projects to offset monetary penalties, if these provide "tangible environmental or public health benefits to the affected community or environment, [are] closely related to the violation being resolved, but [go] beyond what is required under federal, state or local laws."[4] Creative lawyers on all sides of litigation can produce outcomes that advance sustainable development.

4. *Supplemental Environmental Projects (SEPs)*, U.S. ENV'T PROT. AGENCY, https://www.epa.gov/enforcement/supplemental-environmental-projects-seps (last visited Apr. 11, 2022).

d. Advocacy

Advocacy on behalf of sustainable development is another important skill for every lawyer. Of course, it is embedded in litigation and other legal work. But it is also necessary in other contexts. Lawyers using a sustainable development lens comment on proposed regulations and proposed government agency actions; testify before congressional and legislative committees; lobby legislators and government agencies; and present arguments before city councils, zoning hearing boards, and corporate boards. One sustainable development lawyer who left law practice for a period says: "I came back to being involved with the law because I saw that there is an enormous amount of work to do on advocacy." This includes "helping people understand how things are connected and how some things that seem okay are really bad in the long run." Brownfields remediation demonstrates how sustainable development arguments can broaden the range of issues being considered as well as potential solutions. One lawyer worked on a remediation case where the property owner, a refinery, was in bankruptcy. The bankruptcy trustee asked this lawyer to see if it was possible to turn the site into a solar farm. The overall objective, this lawyer explained, was to "actually make money for the estate."

e. Drafting

Drafting is another frequently employed type of work for lawyers engaged in sustainable development. Drafting is a powerful tool for advancing sustainable development because it involves writing the public laws and private agreements that govern the behavior of individuals, businesses, and organizations in specific contexts. This includes drafting proposed statutes and regulations, municipal ordinances representing best practices in sustainability, and private governance agreements for land development (including homeowner associations; commercial associations; and codes, covenants, and restrictions). It also includes editing various disclosure documents. One lawyer helped revise a municipal regulation involving water use and conservation. "In my city, we were charging less on a per-unit basis the more water that was used; we turned it upside down, charging more for greater per-unit water use." Another lawyer who works in human rights and corporate social responsibility explains the range of her firm's drafting activities: "We do everything from policy and standard development to developing contract language and vendor guidelines."

Drafting is more than scrivener's work, and it is not merely legal; it requires an attorney to conceptualize how particular actions to advance sustainable development will work in the real world and to make sure that the legal rules as drafted will work in practice. This in turn requires a solid understanding of the subject matter, which frequently involves matters that are not strictly legal in nature. A lawyer who works on sustainable land use and community planning explains:

> A lot of document drafting is a formality, and a lot of lawyers throw that in for free. They don't realize how much damage can be done with a bad document, because it is so hard to change; once you start subdividing a property, it is possible to destroy a lot of value of property with bad documents. A lot of bad legal writing masks fuzzy thinking. A lot of my work involves looking at a master plan and visualizing it at each stage of development and figuring out what needs to be done at each stage.

f. Negotiation

Negotiation, of course, is a recurring part of law practice. The duty of loyalty requires an attorney to consider not just the position that a client takes or wants to take but also the client's underlying interests. In negotiations, this distinction between position and interest is critical. To take an example from real life, consider a dispute between a married couple about where to go on vacation. The husband wants to go to Colorado, while the wife wants to go to Florida. These destinations represent their positions, and on the surface, they cannot be reconciled. But the reasons for these positions—their underlying interests—provide an opportunity to resolve the conflict. If the husband wants to be in the mountains and the wife wants to be at a beach, they can find a place that has both—say Lake Tahoe.[5] Finding the underlying reason for a person's position will allow the lawyer to help the parties find common ground and, perhaps, a solution that meets the real needs of each party.

The distinction between position and interest is especially important in sustainable development law practice: it is possible that the

5. Roger Fisher, William L. Ury & Bruce Patton, Getting to Yes: Negotiating Agreement without Giving In (1981).

client's position may not be in the client's own best interest or that the client's objectives might be better achieved by pursuing a different approach. A lawyer can provide invaluable assistance to clients by exploring whether there might be better ways to achieve the result sought by the client and exploring other potential benefits not recognized or accounted for by the client. For example, a client may want to quickly obtain necessary permits to build a large solar facility near a residential neighborhood. But acting quickly may not serve the client's interest in putting the proposed facility into operation, particularly if quick action could be interpreted by the neighbors as precipitous and insensitive, leading to citizen opposition and even to time-consuming litigation. If the client has already announced the plan, a lawyer might advise the client that its interests may be better served by fully and thoughtfully addressing concerns that the citizens may have before proceeding further. If the lawyer has a chance to advise the client beforehand, it might be appropriate to suggest that the client not announce the plan until it has first heard from the neighbors and made any appropriate changes.

g. Pro Bono

More and more pro bono legal work is directed toward sustainable development and climate change mitigation. Because sustainable development is a comprehensive framework for ensuring human freedom and well-being, it necessarily demands effectively combating the climate crisis. As a practical matter, the only way to effectively address the climate crisis is to reduce greenhouse gas emissions in a way that also fosters equitable economic development, national security, and job creation—basic elements of sustainable development.

In 2019, the ABA House of Delegates adopted a resolution urging "lawyers to engage in pro bono activities to aid efforts to reduce greenhouse gas emissions and adapt to climate change."[6] In 2020, the International Bar Association—the global counterpart to the ABA—adopted a statement on the climate crisis that urges lawyers to act

6. Am. Bar Ass'n House of Delegates, Res. 111 (2019), https://www.americanbar.org/content/dam/aba/directories/policy/annual-2019/111-annual-2019.pdf.

"on a pro bono, volunteer or reduced fee basis, for those negatively impacted by the climate crisis."[7]

One pro bono opportunity grows out of a 2019 book that describes and analyzes some 1,500 recommended legal tools to reduce greenhouse gas emissions.[8] Federal, state, and local governments, and the private sector, need to adopt and implement such tools if we are to reduce greenhouse gas emissions to net zero or below by 2050. The next stage of this project is drafting these recommendations as model laws that can be proposed, adopted, and implemented in various jurisdictions. More than 20 law firms as well as individual attorneys, law professors, and others are participating in this project on a pro bono basis. These model laws, in turn, are posted (with other resources) on a website created for that purpose.[9]

A striking aspect of this project is the participation of lawyers at all stages of their careers. Many retired attorneys, some of whom have not previously worked in environmental or energy law, including a judge and a recording industry lawyer, help manage this project. First-year associates at law firms also participate, helping to draft model laws pro bono.

h. Other Types of Legal Work

The types of legal work described here do not fully capture the range of skills or types of legal work that may be involved. One lawyer's firm serves as a facilitator for multistakeholder dialogues—a form of collaborative decision-making that engages all actors who have a stake in the decision. This lawyer facilitates dialogues on a variety of issues, including voluntary principles for security and human rights. Other lawyers need to have the ability to work effectively with scientists or engineers on specific projects (e.g., infrastructure design and development). Community service and public education work on sustainable development are also needed.

---

7. Int'l Bar Ass'n, Climate Crisis Statement (2020), https://www.ibanet.org/MediaHandler?id=822c1967-f851-4819-8200-2fe298164922.

8. Legal Pathways to Deep Decarbonization in the United States (Michael B. Gerrard & John C. Dernbach eds., 2019).

9. *Model Laws for Deep Decarbonization in the United States*, Columbia Law Sch. Sabin Ctr. for Climate Change & Widener Univ. Commw. Law Sch. Env't Law & Sustainability Ctr., https://lpdd.org/ (last visited Apr. 11, 2022).

People trained as lawyers can successfully use their skills on behalf of sustainable development in a variety of nonlegal settings. In fact, legal training provides lawyers with skills that others working on a problem or issue may not have. As one lawyer explains:

> The skills that lawyers bring to the table are an ability to communicate orally and in writing better than almost every other professional sector and to critically analyze a situation. I see that over and over again. Some lawyers also have the ability to convene all players, get them to the table to achieve a particular result, and deliver it.

In sum, as reflected in Figure 4.1, legal work for sustainable development does not fall into one or two narrow categories. Instead, it involves a wide variety of different skills that must be applied in a myriad of legal contexts carried out in public and private governance contexts as well as in their personal behaviors.

Figure 4.1 The Difference Maker—Version 3

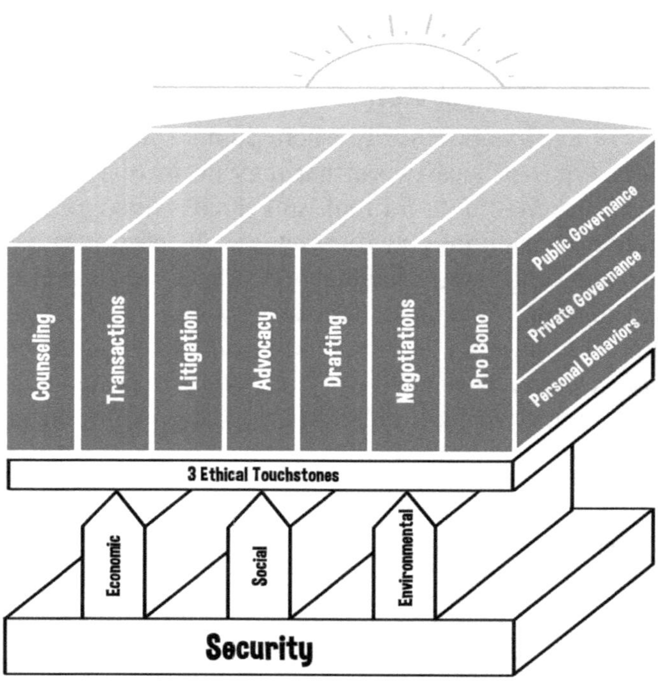

Making a Difference

5

Getting Started on Sustainable Development Leadership

In the first four chapters of this book, we explained the history and meaning of sustainable development, the relevant rules for lawyer conduct, and what sustainable development lawyers do. In this chapter we pivot to what all of this means for you. This chapter explains why leadership (including your leadership) is so important and describes what we mean. Unless and until lawyers as a profession go "all in" on applying the sustainable development lens to their work and their communities, progress toward a sustainable society will be difficult at best. This chapter then provides suggestions for developing your leadership ability on sustainable development.

1. The Importance of Leadership by Lawyers

It is one thing to understand the decision-making process described in Chapters 1 and 2 for generating more sustainable outcomes. It is quite another for the use of that decision-making process to become commonplace. To improve our profession, communities, and society, we need far more lawyers helping their clients and communities make progress toward a sustainable society, and as soon as possible—new lawyers and old, those in private practice and those in public or non-profit practice.

We are moving into a world where business as usual no longer works. The COVID-19 pandemic will not be the last or only shock we will experience in our lifetimes. Climate change will force another set of substantial changes. We need the ability to keep our eye on the big picture and the long term while we navigate these shocks and transitions.

And we need lawyers who can help clients, communities, and society do this important work. It is true, as many have said, that sustainable development requires technology developers, scientists, engineers, planners, and effective political leaders. We agree that each of these is important and believe that each should do more.[1] We make a similar argument here for lawyers.

For decades, too many lawyers have stayed on the sidelines even though society and the legal system upon which it rests have obvious cracks that need to be fixed. Reputational issues, potential conflicts of interest, and other concerns may be some of the barriers to more lawyers taking action. But whatever the case, the consequences of lawyers not effectively adopting the sustainable development decision-making framework are far different today than in earlier times.

America's 1.3 million lawyers have a meaningful role to play in charting a sustainable future because that future depends to no small degree on law and the work that lawyers do. In resolutions adopted in 1991, 2003, and 2013, the American Bar Association House of Delegates recognized the important role lawyers have in realizing sustainable development. In its 2013 resolution, it urged all lawyers "to act in ways that accelerate progress toward sustainability."[2] Do we sit idly by, or do we figure out how to engage wholeheartedly because it's our special responsibility as lawyers to lead the reforms that society needs?

---

1. *See* Jane Lubchenco, *Delivering on Science's Social Contract*, 5 MICH. J. SUSTAINABILITY 95 (2017), https://quod.lib.umich.edu/m/mjs/12333712.0005.106?view=text;rgn=main.

2. Am. Bar Ass'n House of Delegates, Res. 105 (2013), https://www.americanbar.org/content/dam/aba/administrative/office_president/2013_hod_annual_meeting_105.authcheckdam.pdf.

But what does "leadership" mean in this context? In brief, leadership is the ability to work with others to achieve a mutually recognized goal. A well-known text on leadership by Peter Guy Northouse describes leadership as a process whereby one actor influences others in a group to work to achieve shared objectives.[3] James Strock, who was the first secretary of California's Environmental Protection Agency, says: "Twenty-first century leaders inspire others to alter their thoughts and actions, in alignment with an empowering vision."[4] In her book *Lawyers as Leaders*, the late Stanford law professor Deborah Rhode stated that "[l]eadership is a process, not a position, a relationship, not a status."[5] Your relationship with others is critical, and you can exercise leadership regardless of your position in an organization.

You can do this through systems leadership. Systems leadership is needed when no one person or entity is in control. Much of the popular discussion about leadership involves an individual heading up a particular public, private, or nonprofit entity and what that individual needs to do to lead that entity. However, no single entity or individual is in control of sustainable development. For any given public or private decision, the ability to influence outcomes is distributed across a wide range of individuals within an organization and often includes other organizations or persons. Many of these stakeholders, in fact, do not report to the leadership of the organization making the decision or taking the action. These include affected businesses or industries, customers, neighbors, employees, shareholders, nongovernmental organizations, investors, the media, and the public—all of whom are in some sense stakeholders.

The emerging field of systems leadership borrows from many other fields where distributed leadership is key to producing better outcomes.[6] Practically applied, "systems leadership is a set of skills and capacities that any individual or organization can use to catalyze, enable and support the process of systems-level change. It combines

3. Peter Guy Northouse, Leadership: Theory and Practice (8th ed. 2019).

4. James M. Strock, Serve to Lead: Your Transformational 21st Century Leadership System 26 (2010).

5. Deborah L. Rhode, Lawyers as Leaders 203 (2013).

6. Marshall Ganz, *Why Stories Matter: The Art and Craft of Social Change*, Sojourners (Mar. 2009), https://sojo.net/magazine/march-2009/why-stories-matter?action=magazine.article&issue=soj0903&article=why-stories-matter.

collaborative leadership, coalition-building, and systems insight to mobilize innovation and action across a large, decentralized network."[7]

As a 2019 report from Harvard's Corporate Social Responsibility Initiative describes,[8] systems leaders can apply systems leadership principles to influence a wide variety of complex systems—from small ones like a workplace to large ones like a national health care system[9] or our system of justice. The smaller and less complex a system is, the easier it should be to understand the interventions or inputs that will produce a desired set of outcomes.

We will introduce you to a specific systems leadership framework beginning in Chapter 7. But for now, the key things to understand are that systems leadership involves multiple actors throughout any organization and outside it. It also involves collaboration and trust building to set and achieve shared goals. It requires, in short, the kinds of things in which any attorney, at any stage in his or her career, can participate.

We argue that leadership is not simply natural; it can be learned. And whether you are a law student, a young lawyer, or an experienced lawyer, you have already had to demonstrate leadership skills of some sort to get through school and operate in the profession. We hope to help you add to that skill set, contextualizing it for sustainable development.

2. Build Your Sustainable Development Expertise and Own It

This is the single most important requirement for a lawyer who does this work. And of course, it is difficult to lead without the kind of deep knowledge necessary to be taken seriously by others. Thus, a

---

7. Lisa Dreier, David Nabarro & Jane Nelson, *Systems Leadership Can Change the World—But What Exactly Is It?*, World Econ. Forum (Sept. 24, 2019), https://www.weforum.org/agenda/2019/09/systems-leadership-can-change-the-world-but-what-does-it-mean/.

8. Lisa Dreier, David Nabarro & Jane Nelson, Harvard Kennedy Sch. Corp. Resp. Initiative, Systems Leadership for Sustainable Development: Strategies for Achieving Systemic Change (2019), https://www.hks.harvard.edu/sites/default/files/centers/mrcbg/files/Systems%20Leadership.pdf.

9. Charlotte Bigland et al., *Systems Leadership in Practice: Thematic Insights from Three Public Health Case Studies*, 20 BMC Pub. Health 1735 (2020), https://bmcpublichealth.biomedcentral.com/articles/10.1186/s12889-020-09641-1.

starting point is understanding sustainable development, as discussed in Chapters 1 and 2. Increase your understanding of the topic by reading some of the voluminous background information that exists. One lawyer says that expertise in sustainability includes "relevant legal frameworks, best practices, what other companies in the industry are doing in sustainability, and what government policies are relevant." Another emphasizes the importance of mastering the wide variety of issues that will continue to arise in this "quickly trending and developing area."

It is difficult to develop that expertise without a good measure of interest, passion, or enthusiasm for sustainable development. One lawyer explains that "you have to have a genuine interest in it" to understand the environmental, economic, and social facets of any given issue and "all of the different parties that will be impacted." Or as another lawyer explains: "Enthusiasm helps. You have to convince people."

In developing this expertise, you need to figure out how you fit into the big picture of sustainable development. What personal qualities, values, experience, interests, and expertise do you bring to this issue? There is no single "correct answer." First-century scholar Rabbi Hillel famously asked three questions: "If I am not for myself, who is for me? But if I am for my own self [only], what am I? And if not now, when?"[10] The first two questions can at first appear to be about self-interest. They are instead self-regarding questions, helping you identify your own unique personality, skills, values, and experience. Answering those questions will help you define your role in moving toward a more sustainable society. That role—which is unique to you—will provide the foundation for the kind of leadership you exercise with clients, in your law office, in your community, and elsewhere. It is easier to be passionate, enthusiastic, and effective when you have a sense of your role. (We will get to the third question—"And if not now, when?"—at the end of the chapter.)

3. Find the Right Workplace

You can build sustainability expertise by finding a workplace that does this work or is at least open to you doing this work. Some workplaces

10. Pirkei Avot 1:14 (Charles Taylor trans.), https://www.sefaria.org/Pirkei_Avot.1.1?lang=bi.

are clear and explicit about the desirability of this kind of approach. Legal jobs related to sustainability are widespread, even though they are not ordinarily labeled as such. And they exist in virtually every field of law, as we discussed in Chapter 4. If your firm or law office is not currently doing this kind of work, it may be possible for you to take a sustainable development approach anyway. You can, in other words, build a sustainable development approach into nearly any law practice.

One attorney explains the widespread nature of sustainability positions in law practice:

> There is not a sustainability niche as its own niche. Sustainability can, however, be embedded in lots of areas of legal practice. It may come in on a remediation issue or permitting issue. Sustainability can be a significant part of the practice of a real estate lawyer; brownfields law is a perfect example of sustainability. Corporate lawyers have to think about the supply chain. It is not stand alone; it is a skill or competency that people ought to have in a lot of different areas of legal practice. A lawyer who can use knowledge of sustainability effectively—not just spotting issues and telling a client what they can't do but also finding opportunities and being forward looking—that's the skill.

Some law firms are doing more of this work than others; many lawyers and law firms publicly characterize themselves as doing sustainability-related legal work. One growing area of law firm practice is Environmental, Social, and Governance (ESG), which threads together many parts of the sustainable development framework. In 2021, Reuters invited two of us (Dernbach and Bogoshian) to craft a hypothetical ESG scenario for law firms to address and to help evaluate the many law firm responses. The overall quality and thoughtfulness of the responses indicate the growing role that ESG is playing in law firm sustainability practice.[11]

In-house positions with corporations may be particularly suitable for this kind of work, depending on the corporation. Many other workplaces also support sustainability. Positions in government, including

11. Alex Cohen, *We Put These ESG Lawyers to the Test*, Reuters (July 28, 2021), https://www.reuters.com/legal/legalindustry/we-put-these-esg-lawyers-test-2021-07-26/.

municipalities, may also be good places to advance sustainable development work, particularly if the municipality or other governmental entity is already committed to sustainable development. Another option is nongovernmental organizations oriented toward sustainable development. These organizations may involve the practice of law, including litigation. But it is also possible to use legal and advocacy skills in contexts where one is not strictly practicing law. "These jobs are few and far between," one lawyer says, "but you are advantaged if you have a legal background, because some of what you touch is regulatory in nature."

Even when a law office is not outwardly committed to sustainable development, many lawyers who do sustainability-related legal work have essentially created their own jobs, with the tacit or explicit approval of their law office. A corporate social responsibility lawyer says, "A lot of people who are in this space created their own jobs. It requires a lot of persistence and resilience." Another says that if you want to work on climate change, "jobs are where you create them." One lawyer advises: "Take what is otherwise a traditional environmental or real estate, land use, or insurance job and figure out a way to bring these ideas into your work and push the envelope."

If you want to proceed in this way, it may help to first discuss your goals with a senior partner or other manager. You can explain that approaching legal representations with a sustainable development focus can add value for you and your clients.

In these settings, you will likely find yourself proceeding on a client-by-client basis. Some clients may be open to considering a sustainable development approach, and others may not or may limit sustainability to a discrete set of issues. Many practicing lawyers who do sustainability-related legal work do not spend all of their time on this work. It may represent only a quarter or half of their time. In a work setting like this, you need to be comfortable with the tradeoffs that this entails. For example, you may feel passionate about the work you do for one particular client or one specific matter but uncomfortable with the nature of the work you do for other clients or matters. Of course, as discussed in Chapter 3, you must be willing and able to work competently on both. And your willingness to represent a particular client does not constitute your own personal endorsement of the activities of that client. Being able to help some clients work toward sustainable development at least some of the time could be satisfying. And your ability to produce tangible results through integrated decision-making for these clients could attract other clients.

A creative lawyer should almost always be able to bring sustainable development into his or her work. If not, maybe it is time to start looking for another place to work.

4. Build Sustainable Development Expertise in Fields That Are Relevant to Your Clients

You should, of course, have a solid understanding of what your client does and what laws govern its activities and operations. But as we have seen, sustainable development would change in significant ways the "business as usual" trajectory for most clients. It also likely implicates additional or different laws. Understanding these different practices and additional laws will give you the expertise needed to add value for clients.

One way to understand how sustainable development would change business as usual is to see what similarly situated clients, or peers, are already doing on sustainable development. In nearly every field, leading companies, businesses, and other entities engage in best practices for sustainable development. Learn what those best practices are. If you have clients who design and construct buildings, for example, you should learn about the Leadership in Energy and Environmental Design (LEED) program run by the U.S. Green Building Council. Under this program, buildings can be certified as green buildings if they are built and operated with certain energy-saving and environmental attributes.[12] Clients who seek LEED certification are doing something that is not business as usual, although LEED certification is becoming much more common. In fact, some lawyers have earned LEED credentials to enhance their expertise in green building.[13] Other lawyers develop a working knowledge of the voluntary corporate reporting and disclosure standards described in Chapter 1. You may also need to develop your scientific or technological understanding of particular fields relevant to your clients. Be sure, as you do

12. *LEED Rating System*, U.S. Green Bldg. Council, https://www.usgbc.org/leed (last visited Apr. 11, 2022).

13. *LEED Professional Credentials*, U.S. Green Bldg. Council, https://www.usgbc.org/credentials (last visited Apr. 11, 2022).

this, that you are using the best available evidence or science and are not gathering false or misleading information.

Law relevant to sustainable development, as we have seen, is also not necessarily the same as the law required for business as usual. A LEED green building certification, for instance, is not ordinarily required by law, and so learning about this is in addition to learning other legal requirements. Green building also brings with it a specialized set of legal issues.[14] In other cases, existing statutes have sustainability consequences of which clients may be unaware, as in the case of federal and state tax incentives and grant programs available for energy efficiency and renewable energy. For climate change in particular, it is important to keep up with the wide range of legal developments at the local, state, federal, and international levels. You may not be able to bill clients for all of the time required to develop this expertise, but building the expertise will better enable you to provide legal and other advice that is directly relevant to your clients.

5. Build Special Skills That Are Essential for Sustainable Development Work

Sustainable development work in law practice is a lot like legal work in general. It requires the use of all the skills that lawyers need generally. The following skills, however, are particularly important for legal work in sustainable development.

a. Ability to Listen Well

Many people are interested in doing sustainability-related legal work because they want to convince others of the value of this approach. But it is first important to listen to your client. Whether or not the client is explicitly oriented toward sustainable development, listening helps you understand how the client sees problems, what the client cares about, and what the client wants. This is not only about simply listening; it is also about asking good questions to clarify meaning or check assumptions. One lawyer says, "The key thing is hearing what

---

14. *The Legal and Business Case for LEED Certification in the Post-Recession World*, AM. BAR ASS'N (Jan. 31, 2011), https://www.americanbar.org/groups/business_law/publications/blt/2011/01/03_mergens/.

people really want so you can find a solution for everyone." Another spends a lot of time listening to clients, "trying to figure out various approaches to address a particular problem."

b. Open-Mindedness, Curiosity, and Creativity

These qualities overlap, and many attorneys explain themselves in this way. A lawyer who works with developers says: "I am constantly questioning why architects, engineers, or planners do something in a certain way, so we can unlock creative ways of meeting their goals while accomplishing those goals in a more sustainable fashion." Another describes intellectual flexibility, imagination, and creativity as essential:

> That's why I like the work. We need to develop new answers to questions. It is not a field for lawyers who are comfortable doing the same thing year after year with the same forms. It is a field for people who are prepared to invent or be creative. Yet as a counterpoint, you can't be operating in the ionosphere. You must be realistic and pragmatic.

A good example of this creativity is provided by a lawyer in private practice with a municipal client. The lawyer proposed a public–private partnership to enable the city to combine ground source geothermal energy recovery with subsurface stormwater recharge basins. Because of the creative approach of having the project privately owned but operated on behalf of the city, the owner was able to take advantage of tax credits, and the city was able to take advantage of private capital.

One lawyer who counsels many small companies says it is not just necessary for the attorney to be creative. The attorney must also have "a love of working with creative people. Some of the people I work with are the coolest people ever. Most of my developers are 'mom and pops.' They want to make money, but they see themselves as stewards of the land and they want to create something enduring."

c. Patience and Persistence

It is important to be patient with clients, particularly when they are resistant or do not yet understand sustainable development concepts, principles, and applications. You need to be prepared to explain, translate, and clarify issues related to sustainability and respond effectively to questions. One lawyer says: "You have to keep winnowing down the negative conversation about why we would do that, and what are the benefits to us." Being patient, however, does not mean you should give up on bringing the sustainable development lens to your work. If a client or situation does not at first seem amenable to this kind of analysis, try to find other ways to approach using it.

Patience with yourself is important, as you learn these skills. Patience is also important as you cope with the personal stress of climate change and other threats. It is essential for you to be in community with others with whom you can share your experience and stresses.

d. Ability to Think Big Picture and Long Term Based on the Best Available Evidence

Sustainable development requires lawyers to approach problems from a broader perspective than ordinary decision-making. The three pillars of sustainability, one lawyer says, require "a much broader lens"—the ability to "connect seemingly disparate ideas and work areas"—and to break down silos. This kind of thinking, of course, must be based on the best available evidence, including the best science. From this perspective, for example, legal advice on forest protection is not just about the forest itself but also about economic development and community protection. Another attorney describes "an ability to think about things at a meta or systemic level and then drill down to components of that to more granular levels and move back and forth between systemic and granular levels."

An attorney must think long term—about "what the world is going to be like in 50 or 60 years," says another who works with Native Americans. This attorney explained that Native Americans "introduced me to the idea of thinking seven generations ahead." This principle is a core value of the Haudenosaunee (Iroquois) philosophy and is widely shared among Native Americans.[15]

15. *Values*, Haudenosaunee Confederacy, https://www.haudenosauneeconfederacy.com/values/ (last visited Apr. 11, 2022); David E. Wilkins, *How to Honor the Seven Generations*, Indian Country Today (Sept. 12, 2018), https://indiancountrytoday.com/archive/how-to-honor-the-seven-generations.

e. Knowing Your Boundaries

Even though much of this chapter reviews ways in which lawyers can lead more widespread use of the sustainable development framework in decision-making, we recognize that generalizing about recommended practices for lawyers is risky and difficult; lawyers operate in a wide variety of different roles and contexts. We also recognize the risks associated with going too far or in the wrong direction in trying to apply this approach in your practice.

To be sure, lawyer leadership often includes inserting creative and productive tension within work situations to produce better, more sustainable outcomes. Still, we do not want lawyers getting fired or penalized for failing to follow a thoughtful and context-appropriate approach. Knowing your boundaries means understanding what attorney behavior is considered appropriate by your colleagues and clients and generally following those norms. If you push too hard or in the wrong way, you may get into trouble. And yet at the same time, if you don't push hard enough, you may not be heard or be an effective change maker. Figuring out what is just right in your situation is part of the challenge. If you are unsure what these boundaries are on a particular point, ask an ethics expert, mentor, or other legal professional you trust for advice.

Even though there may be risks, lawyers can and must bring a sustainable development decision-making process into their work, producing better outcomes for colleagues, clients, and communities. If you respect the boundaries of your employment situation in doing so, you are likely to increase your stature with colleagues and clients, rather than decrease it. You are also likely to be more effective.

6. Learn, Engage, and Network

Find out what other lawyers in your field, your community, and your organization are doing on sustainable development and engage and build networks with them. Wherever you are on your journey of applying the sustainable development lens to your work, you are not alone. Whatever your practice area—real estate, insurance, corporate law, estate planning, land use law, environmental law, energy law, or any other practice area—there are lawyers who are doing sustainability work. Meet them as soon as possible through your work, through bar associations or various nongovernmental organizations, or by simply contacting them. Similarly, whatever community you are living and working in, find lawyers with similar interests or expertise. Thanks to the telephone, internet, and social media, it is easy to get started because no one is too far away. People you reach out to are likely to be an invaluable source of information and expertise, as well as support and feedback. As your expertise and networks increase, share what you have learned, as appropriate, with clients and others. We explain how to do that in greater detail in the remainder of this book.

This chapter has provided basic advice on getting started in sustainable development leadership in the practice of law. As the illustration below shows, leadership requires you to begin applying these practices and then persuading others to do the same. Which gets us back to Rabbi Hillel's third question: "And if not now, when?" Given the challenging problems in front of us and the opportunities they present, the only answer to this question is "now."

6

Giving Effective Advice on Sustainable Development

In Chapter 5, we moved from explaining basic principles to explaining what they mean for you. In that chapter, we discussed the importance of sustainability leadership and how you can get started in applying sustainable development to your legal work. In this chapter, we set out four principles for giving effective advice on sustainable development issues, drawing on what experienced lawyers have learned in doing this work. We all can and should be sustainable development lawyers.

1. Before Giving Any Advice, Understand Your Client's Goals, Orientation, and Business

Wherever you work, you can't give effective advice on sustainable development issues unless you know a lot about what your client wants and the kind of work or business your client conducts. To get answers to these questions, you should communicate with your client and study the client's work or business based on online materials, personal observation, and other sources. In addition, learn what you can about what, if anything, your client has already done to advance sustainability. It is also essential to develop a good rapport with your client. When you have a trusting relationship with, and understand, your client, you can align your sustainable development advice to what your client actually wants, and you are more likely to be taken seriously.

A contrasting style, which is rarely effective, is to give your client advice on sustainability-related issues without having first done this preparatory work. If you do that, you are likely to get a lot of things wrong and also offend your client.

Part of learning about your client is understanding the different roles that people play in your client's organization and the different perspectives they bring to the table. This is particularly true when the organization has people whose job is to promote sustainable development. Sometimes legal advice is best directed at those within an organization who can use it to advocate a particular outcome to more senior management.

Lawyers who apply sustainable development often begin with basic questions. One attorney says, "I mostly just ask questions: How important is sustainability to you? Do you simply want to comply with the law or do you want to be aspirational?" An energy lawyer simply points out to clients that "there are other ways and places they can go that serve them at other levels. It is just part of conversation, not where I am preaching."

It is also helpful to understand what particular issues the client does and does not care about. One lawyer first understands which issues the client is sensitive to—for example, reputational risk, litigation risk, or social responsibility—and uses these issues to explain sustainable development.

An attorney who works with many multinational corporations does not broadly raise sustainability-related issues with clients but rather sees the sustainability framework as akin to medicine, "looking at the patient holistically." This attorney says:

> When a client comes to me with a problem that opens a portal to sustainability analysis, I will look at it through that portal. Then we don't have twelve discussions about the same symptom—for example, worker dust inhalation claims at different facilities over time. That may be indicative that the company is using materials that are not sustainable or sourced sustainably, and alternatives may exist that will eliminate the entire issue.

2. Explain Sustainable Development Options in Terms of Significant or Material Risks and Opportunities

Once you recognize that it is appropriate to raise sustainable development issues and understand what your client cares about, the challenge is to explain sustainability options to your client in ways that your client will take seriously. As Chapter 4 explains, the sustainable development framework reveals a wider range of potential impacts (particularly environmental, social, and economic impacts) from a decision—positive and negative—than a client may previously have considered.

A first step, then, is to understand the opportunities and risks of a proposal or project in the manner described in Chapter 4 and share what you learn with your client. That will enable your client to shape a decision or project in a way that maximizes benefits and reduces risks. Often, understanding the risks and opportunities requires outreach to the affected community. As one attorney explains, it might be better to "spend more time and money now" on community outreach "to save a lot more time and money later by achieving a sustainable result."

Here is an illustrative list of opportunities and risk avoidance measures:

- Saving money via operational improvements (e.g., energy efficiency, adoption of new technologies, changing business practices)
- Reducing regulatory compliance costs that apply to less sustainable activities by employing best practices on sustainable development
- Anticipating and avoiding costly regulatory violations
- Anticipating and avoiding costly litigation
- Anticipating and preparing for inevitable challenges like climate disruption, heat waves, fires, floods, earthquakes, and pandemics
- Recruiting and retaining top people who would rather work for a company dedicated to advancing sustainable development
- Investing in worker safety protections and benefits to reduce worker compensation costs and increase employee loyalty and productivity
- Adopting and implementing meaningful diversity, equity, and inclusion practices
- Attracting new customers by building a brand backed by authentic sustainability practices
- Creating new revenue generating products and services that result from applying more sustainable practices

Of course, as noted in Chapter 4, the most significant risks and opportunities deserve the greatest consideration and are most likely to affect the final decision. But significant in what way? The risks and opportunities of sustainable development, of course, depend on what goods or services the client is producing and how it is producing them or where the client is planning to locate a particular facility. As one environmental attorney explains:

> I put sustainability issues into the context of risk within their industry if they do not address these issues and opportunities they could realize if they addressed these issues. Perhaps for some industries, if one markets a product that has green components (such as household cleaners that are greener), they can capture greater market share.

Sometimes, the risks involve costs of compliance with existing laws. A lawyer who works on hazardous waste issues raises sustainability "whenever we are looking at a waste stream. I ask: 'Why are you generating this? Do you want to have to deal with these rules?'" By not generating that waste stream, the client may significantly reduce compliance costs under federal and state hazardous waste laws.

Climate change risks and opportunities are increasingly important. A land use attorney explains:

> Today we are telling people not to build in high hazard areas so you don't get flooded. There are risks of climate change that are being picked up by conservative markets—banks, lenders, secondary mortgage markets. If a client is not assessing these risks—and our job is due diligence as lawyers—then I'm seeing an opportunity that perhaps others have not opened their eyes to.

At other times, risks and opportunities are more obvious when one looks at a client's peers. Lawyers who work on sustainable development issues often have several clients who work in the same economic sector or business and are in a particularly good position to explain to clients what their peers are doing on sustainability. Sometimes, one lawyer says, clients "have not yet perceived a risk that we have seen in the history of other companies in the same sector, or they don't have programs that their competitors do. This is also true for business opportunities."

And sometimes the sustainable development framework brings to light a problem that might otherwise have been missed. A land use and development attorney says clients often come to lawyers when something the clients want has simply "gone wrong or is not happening." This lawyer explains:

> They may not identify the issue as a sustainable development issue, but it is clear to us that it is. Why do people have so little disposable income in downtown? Part of the answer is that they are spending too much money on transportation and not enough on housing. So we work on transit-oriented development.

The broader sustainable development frame is also valuable in dealing with stakeholders. One environmental attorney habitually asks clients: "Can't we make this look better for everybody by doing (fill in the blank)?"

Whatever preferences your client may have, there is also an objective definition of what is significant, and it is backed by law, at least for some kinds of clients. The term "materiality" is commonly used to understand what "significant" means, particularly in the business context. Traditionally, the term is used to decide which financial information publicly traded companies must disclose to their boards and shareholders as well as the public. According to the U.S. Supreme Court, "[a]n omitted fact is material if there is a substantial likelihood that a reasonable shareholder would consider it important in deciding how to vote."[1] "Put another way, there must be a substantial likelihood that the disclosure of the omitted fact would have been viewed by the reasonable investor as having significantly altered the 'total mix' of information made available."[2] Publicly traded companies, for example, must publicly disclose "material pending legal proceedings" as well as expenditures that materially affect their financial condition.[3] Under state corporate laws, companies owe similar duties of disclosure to their boards, whether they are publicly traded or not.

Of course, the most obvious material risks and opportunities are expressly economic or financial. Yet it does not take much imagination to see that environmental and social risks and opportunities can also have significant financial consequences. And through an even wider lens, involving the triple bottom line of economic, social, and environmental benefits, risks and opportunities can be material even if their primary impact is on the social and environmental parts of the bottom line. This latter understanding of materiality is not (yet) part of our law, but the law is headed in that direction.

3. Be Prudent in Your Explanations

Raising sustainable development issues with clients can present risks for lawyers—some would say a minefield. This is particularly true for younger or less experienced lawyers who do not have a long

---

1. TSC Indus., Inc. v. Northway, Inc., 426 U.S. 438, 449 (1976).
2. *Id.*
3. George S. Georgiev, *Too Big to Disclose: Firm Size and Materiality Blindspots in Securities Regulation*, 64 UCLA L. Rev. 602, 606–07 (2017).

relationship with their clients. At the same time, raising these issues may offer these lawyers opportunities to not only carry out their ethical obligations described in Chapter 3 but, in so doing, also help clients in ways they did not expect and teach clients a perspective that is likely to have lasting value.

Interestingly, many lawyers make these arguments without mentioning sustainability, sustainable development, or climate change. Some lawyers have found that clients will not listen to an explanation based on climate change but will listen to explanations based on energy efficiency or cost savings. Other lawyers consciously avoid using "sustainability":

> I have lots of sustainability conversations in which the word "sustainability" never comes up—such as about governance, supply chains—but that are based on sustainability as it is properly understood. People hire lawyers, not preachers, and no one wants to be preached at. You can make a lot of good medicine that will go down with the right amount of sugar.

A green building and community development lawyer explains the dynamics of such conversations:

> A lot of times I tell them how to save money, how it will give them an economic advantage in the marketplace. We talk about almost everything, except "that is the right thing to do and will save the world." That doesn't mean I don't have clients that believe that. If I have to persuade them, though, these other aspects get emphasized. . . . The challenge here is to convince a client of both intrinsic benefits (lower cost, increase in tenants, lower operating costs, higher retention rate for tenants) and extrinsic benefits (that might benefit the community or the environment and would mean that the community is more likely to support your project).

This lawyer adds that there are often limits in how far an attorney can go in arguing for the intrinsic benefits of sustainable development:

> Some clients are wary of attorneys who pitch intrinsic benefits. The clients see the attorneys as engaging in advocacy. They worry that you are advocating something and if they say no, your heart won't be in advocating for their position. I had one client who hired me because I pushed back against what

> he proposed, but I would move his project forward whether I won or lost our internal arguments. He didn't buy all of the things I suggested as sustainable, but he bought a lot of them.

As this lawyer suggested, being prudent enhances your likelihood of success but does not guarantee it.

4. Consider Preparation of Special Sustainable Development Templates for Particular Contexts

When the opportunity to discuss sustainable development with clients arises, many lawyers have "menus" of issues, tools, and options to share with them. Options include various tax incentives, rebates, and grant programs. Tools often include specific methods or areas of expertise that lawyers have developed to address particular problems. This approach gives you an opportunity to create specialized approaches to sustainable development that can attract and retain clients. One lawyer presents "social entrepreneur clients" with a "menu of sustainability choices," including rules of corporate citizenship, writing into the company's bylaws how the company treats people and the planet, and getting needed sustainability certifications. A real estate development lawyer who has gained expertise in solar energy and other aspects of sustainable real estate development has a standard approach:

> The client may buy an industrial building with a big roof. I say you can put solar panels on the roof, and you can make money. That starts the conversation, and the client gets an 8 percent return on its investment. Then the client comes back and says: "What else is in your bag of tricks?" And then I talk about LEDs [which are up to 90 percent more energy efficient than incandescent lights]. And that is how you make converts. This is how you get their attention.

This chapter has described basic principles for giving effective advice to clients on sustainable development. We must all be sustainable development lawyers now. As with other aspects of client counseling, some trial and error is involved, and you will get better with practice.

7

Sustainable Development Lawyers as Systems Leaders in Legal Work

To be truly transformative, lawyers must be able to do more than use sustainable development in their practice. Lawyers must also become "systems leaders." In this chapter, we explain a particular systems leadership framework and then illustrate how lawyers can use this framework in doing legal work. In the next two chapters, we show how to use this framework to exercise lawyer leadership in other contexts.

In Chapter 5, we introduced systems leadership as a way of collaborating with others to achieve shared goals. The first step in applying systems leadership is adoption of a particular systems leadership framework. We use Harvard's CLEAR framework[1] in the hypothetical stories

1. Lisa Dreier, David Nabarro & Jane Nelson, Harvard Kennedy Sch. Corp. Resp. Initiative, Systems Leadership for Sustainable Development: Strategies for Achieving Systemic Change (2019), https://www.hks.harvard.edu/sites/default/files/centers/mrcbg/files/Systems%20Leadership.pdf.

that follow because it adopts many elements of other system leadership frameworks and is easy to follow. This framework has five parts:[2]

1. **Convene and Commit.** "Key stakeholders engage in moderated dialogue to address a complex issue of mutual concern. They define shared interests and goals and commit to working together in new ways to create systemic change."[3]
2. **Look and Learn.** Stakeholders conduct a process called system mapping that looks at how variables interact over time and form patterns of behaviors across a system.[4] By doing so, they "jointly build a shared understanding of the components, actors, dynamics, and influences that create the system and its current outcomes."[5] They generate new insights and ideas about where more sustainable practices can supplant current unsustainable processes.
3. **Engage and Energize.** Diverse stakeholders engage through "continuous communication to build trust, commitment, innovation, and collaboration. Inspiration, incentives, and milestones help drive progress and maintain momentum."[6]
4. **Act with Accountability.** "Shared goals and principles set the direction of the initiative, while measurement frameworks are developed to help track progress. Coordination and governance structures can be developed as initiatives mature."[7]
5. **Review and Revise.** "Stakeholders review progress regularly and adapt the initiative where needed. Adopting an agile, flexible, innovative, and learning-centered approach allows for evolution and experimentation."[8]

---

2. *Id.* at 4.
3. *Id.*
4. Erin Gray & Charlie Bloch, *Systems Mapping—A Vital Ingredient for Successful Partnerships*, World Res. Inst. (Aug. 17, 2020), https://www.wri.org/insights/insider-systems-mapping-vital-ingredient-successful-partnerships#:~:text=Broadly%20speaking%2C%20systems%20mapping%20is,partners%20on%20the%20same%20page.
5. Dreier, Nabarro & Nelson, *supra* note 1, at 4.
6. *Id.*
7. *Id.*
8. *Id.*

This chapter provides a hypothetical story using the CLEAR framework to demonstrate what systems leadership for sustainability can look like in the practice of law.

Ali is an associate at a midsized law firm that provides numerous types of legal services to business clients. Ali reports to Hannah, a partner who has been at the firm for almost 20 years. For most of the five years Ali has been doing this work, he has considered it pretty far afield from his undergraduate interests. At different points in his journey he had thought of being a teacher, or a park ranger, or even a marine scientist. Ali went to law school figuring that he'd get some experience, make some money, and then "make a difference" later in his career.

Ali has excelled at transactional work, especially supply chain contracting. One of his clients was Brighton Tractor Supply Company (BTSC).[9] BTSC is a publicly traded American company with more than $1 billion in annual revenue. It provides goods and services to industrial farm and factory operations across the country. Its supply chains are multifaceted and international. BTSC also has hazardous waste legal issues resulting from improper storage and disposal of used batteries returned to them in their rental and service business. Ali's fellow associate, Jenny, dealt with those issues.

One day, Ali attended a Minimum Continuing Legal Education (MCLE) session on how supply chain contracts could produce better outcomes for clients if companies demanded that their suppliers incorporate into their contracts certain Environmental, Social, and Governance (ESG) terms. Ali had heard about ESG in the past but hadn't given it much thought. But now he absorbed the material in earnest. Not only did Ali learn about how companies could save money with smarter supply chain contracts, but he also became excited to see how he might weave his contracting expertise with additional services that could help BTSC and other clients and also expand the firm's business.

Since Jenny was also doing legal work for BTSC, Ali shared his new enthusiasm for applied sustainability and the MCLE program with her. Jenny liked what she heard and suggested they also bring in another associate, Remo, who was providing corporate governance

9. This hypothetical was the basis for a Reuters survey of law firm Environmental, Social, and Governance (ESG) practices. For the article and the law firm responses, see Alex Cohen, *We Put These ESG Lawyers to the Test*, Reuters (July 28, 2021), https://www.reuters.com/legal/legalindustry/we-put-these-esg-lawyers-test-2021-07-26/.

advice to BTSC. After sharing notes on what they were learning, Remo said that he too was learning a bit about ESG and wanted to do more to figure out how to apply it with clients. Remo said that one of BTSC's vice presidents had told him that BTSC was getting questions from its board and customers about how sustainable the company is. In response, BTSC was starting to consider having one of its vice presidents codesignated as BTSC's Chief Sustainability Officer.

1. Legal Work: Convene and Commit

Jenny suggested that they use the CLEAR systems leadership framework to guide their efforts. She explained that every client business is an organizational "system" in its own right, operating in a larger system that produces products, services, jobs, profits, and other outputs. After some clarifying conversations, Ali and Remo thought that the framework made sense. As such, all three agreed to spend some nonbillable time thinking about how to integrate sustainable development into their legal support for BTSC using the CLEAR framework.

2. Legal Work: Look and Learn

They started by assessing BTSC's legal needs with a new and different lens, a sustainable development lens. Knowing the people at BTSC as he did, Ali knew that they thought the supply chain contracting issues were nothing but a burden. That is, they often asked Ali the same question, in different ways: how can we get the best financial terms possible? Because of what he was learning, Ali now knew that BTSC's narrow view was causing it to miss many money-making and sustainability opportunities. Ali drafted a one-page list of existing supply chain contracts coming up for renewal that could include ESG provisions, many of which could also produce cost savings. He recognized that inserting ESG supply chain provisions might increase short-term costs in certain cases and could even lead to some suppliers not renewing their contracts. To enable him to better address the likely resistance, he produced a memorandum and supporting material making the case for more sustainable supply chain contracting.

As Jenny looked at Ali's list, she saw a couple of battery supply contracts and began to think about how having better battery supply chain contracts and/or better battery supply chain contractors could have helped BTSC avoid the $375,000 in fines and cleanup costs it was facing from the state's Department of the Environment. Jenny was helping defend BTSC in this case. Because the evidence of liability was overwhelming, she had already advised BTSC's general counsel to settle. Jenny knew that the state's prosecutor might consider "offsetting" money spent to prevent problems like this from happening again as a way to reduce penalties BTSC would otherwise have to pay. So she suggested to Ali that they focus on battery suppliers, both those involved in the case and others. Her idea was to use new contract terms that could prevent the problems that led to the litigation and try to use these new terms to reduce BTSC's likely fines.

Remo, meanwhile, was thinking more broadly about what ESG could mean for the firm. Over the years he had learned that more enterprises and even law firms were using ESG reporting to inform important decisions. Even though he knew it was in the early days in reporting reliable ESG information,[10] he also knew that the sooner the law firm began to do this work, the sooner it could benefit clients. Remo figured that describing litigation prevention in the language and metrics of ESG—and using it as an example for how all of BTSC's activities could be explained and ultimately measured and reported in an ESG reporting system—might also be good for the law firm.

Ali, Jenny, and Remo knew they had lots to learn about ESG and how integrated decision-making could apply to BTSC, not to mention other clients. They decided to drill down into this situation by adopting a three-part plan. Ali would work on developing better supply chain contracts for batteries. Jenny would figure out how to use this work to resolve the civil enforcement claim. And Remo would develop a proposal to BTSC to use ESG throughout its supply chain contracting and perhaps throughout its organization.

3. Legal Work: Engage and Energize

As Ali, Jenny, and Remo's "moonlighting" work continued, Ali worried that the partner he worked for, Hannah, would frown upon any

10. *SASB Standards & Other ESG Frameworks: The Sustainability Reporting Ecosystem*, Sustainability Acct. Standards Bd., https://www.sasb.org/about/sasb-and-other-esg-frameworks/ (last visited Apr. 12, 2022).

new approach to existing work that might be perceived as leading to fewer billable hours. Jenny agreed that partner issues could become a concern, so she suggested that they talk to another partner she worked for, Harry. She set up the meeting.

At their meeting, Harry revealed that at a recent partner meeting, he had brought up the idea of sustainability for the operations of the firm itself and in how they do their law work. The partners encouraged Harry to come up with some ideas for moving ahead. After listening intently to the work that Ali, Jenny, and Remo were doing for BTSC and their thinking on how sustainable development could add value for the client, Harry offered to make their BTSC work a pilot project that he would oversee. Their work would be used as an example for doing similar things for other clients. If the three of them agreed, he would agree to talk to Hannah and any other partners to explain what was happening and provide management support. Harry added that he needed to be informed in advance of key steps along the way. Ali, Jenny, and Remo agreed.

Empowered by Harry's support, Jenny suggested that they set up weekly check-in meetings and monthly email progress reports. They reached out to a diverse set of ESG stakeholders who could advise them on their project and help them build expertise. One of those stakeholders was at the nonprofit organization called the Sustainable Accounting Standards Board (SASB).[11] SASB sets standards for reporting sustainability information that is material to companies, their investors, and other stakeholders. Through SASB and others they discovered a whole system of support that could help them on their journey. Of particular interest to Remo was knowing ESG has been receiving attention within many companies and law firms, particularly as a means for meeting corporate compliance responsibilities.[12]

At the same time, they each worked on the three-part plan described earlier. Ali's part, investigating better supply chain contracts, led him to look at the growing shift toward electric vehicles. Ali learned that the U.S. federal government has sponsored a public–private partnership, the REMADE Institute, to accelerate the recovery, reuse, and

---

11. About *Us*, Sustainability Acct. Standards Bd., https://www.sasb.org/about/ (last visited Apr. 12, 2022).

12. Thomas Riesenberg, *To Unlock ESG Value, Look to Compliance and Beyond*, Sustainability Acct. Standards Bd. (Oct. 22, 2020), https://www.sasb.org/blog/recent-articles-to-unlock-esg-value-look-to-compliance-and-beyond/.

remanufacturing of energy-intensive materials, including materials in batteries.[13] Ali contacted the institute and found an attorney who shared samples of supply chain contracting provisions for suppliers of batteries that he could use to increase the recycling, recovery, reuse, and remanufacturing of BTSC's batteries. Ali calculated that changing BTSC's existing supply chain contracts to include some recycling, recovery, reuse, and remanufacturing of batteries BTSC sold would result in legal and transactional costs of at least an estimated $100,000. Ali shared what he learned with Jenny and Remo.

For her part, Jenny used this information to suggest a way of resolving the BTSC enforcement matter. After consulting with Harry and Hannah, she sent BTSC's general counsel a letter proposing that they embed the $100,000 battery supply chain costs as an offset to fines BTSC would have to pay to resolve the hazardous waste litigation.

And for his part, Remo used this information to develop a proposal that BTSC adopt ESG for its entire organization. With the help of ESG experts and other information, Remo put the battery value chain example into an ESG "before and after" comparison to showcase how previously unrevealed and positive outcomes can be identified with ESG analysis. That is, as one example using ESG metrics, Remo could show how the higher costs of past practices with old supply chain contracts (including the costs of hazardous waste fines) compared to better outcomes expected from the new supply chain contracts.

4. Legal Work: Act with Accountability

They continued to present their progress along the way every month to Harry. They set up a computer drive folder to share and comment on each other's work and to track progress. As their work matured, they had ups and downs with different leaders at BTSC and within the law firm. Hannah at times was disgruntled. Harry and the progress the three were making mostly assuaged her concerns.

13. The REMADE Inst., https://remadeinstitute.org/ (last visited Apr. 12, 2022).

5. Legal Work: Review and Revise

When the financial and economic success of the pilot project became clear, Harry asked the three to present their work to the partners. They all recognized that whatever lessons were being learned would need to be adapted to the firm's many different legal contexts and clients. Nonetheless, they also knew they were off to a good start in showcasing an example of sustainable development in the practice of law, as an approach to be applied throughout the firm and the profession.

This story and Figure 7.1 illustrate some of the ways that the CLEAR systems leadership framework can be applied in the legal workplace and in law practice. In the next two chapters we illustrate how systems leadership can be applied in law firm operations and in communities.

Figure 7.1 Difference Maker—Version 4

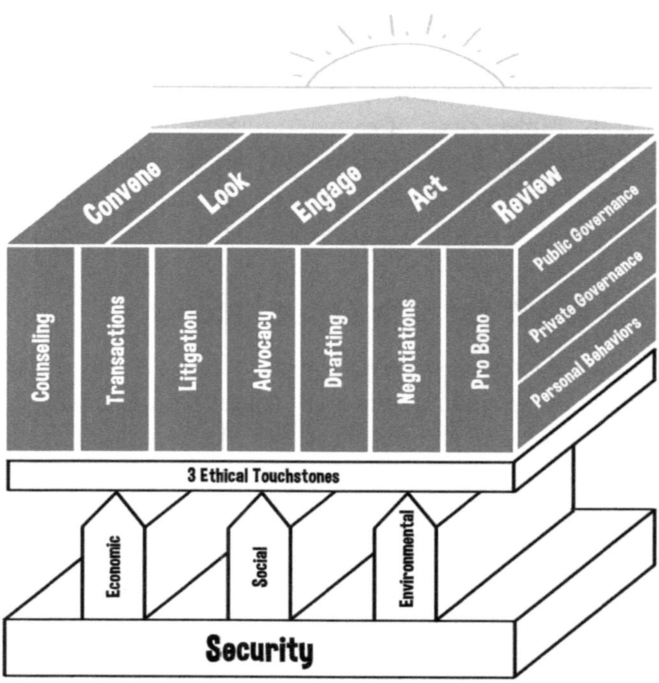

8

Sustainable Development Lawyers as Systems Leaders in the Workplace

The CLEAR systems leadership framework explained in Chapter 7 is useful in settings other than doing legal work. It can also be used to move toward sustainability in the workplace. Here again we use a hypothetical example.

Anna is an associate in a law firm who wants to succeed at the firm and also address climate change in some way. She is not sure what her colleagues and superiors know about sustainable development, nor does she know their commitment to reducing greenhouse gas emissions. She does know that her firm has a problem with recruitment and retention of young associates; she has been asked to speak to prospective hires about working at the firm. Anna read this guide and came across a reference to the California Lawyers Association Model Law Office Sustainability Guidelines (CLAS Guidelines).[1]

1. *Model Law Office Sustainability Guidelines*, CAL. LAWS. ASS'N, https://calawyers.org/environmental-law/model-law-office-sustainability-guidelines/ (last visited Apr. 12, 2022). Other state bar associations have similar guidelines. *See, e.g.*, *Pennsylvania*

The guidelines include 15 sets of more sustainable practices in a law office, including reduced paper use, reuse of equipment and supplies, reduced toxic chemicals, reduced water and energy usage, use of sustainable products and services, recycling, use of renewable energy, and sustainability-related public service.[2] (In the illustration on the next page, a law firm is directly employing solar energy.) Anna did not live or work in California, and her state bar association had not yet developed any kind of sustainability guidelines for lawyers. But it seemed to her that she could get started on becoming more of a sustainability leader herself by getting her firm to adopt some form of the CLAS Guidelines. In addition, there was one sustainable practice she knew about that was not listed in the CLAS Guidelines—minimizing air travel. Anna knew from additional research that commercial air travel accounts for a significant part of greenhouse gas emissions.[3]

During the pandemic, almost everyone at her firm came to realize that lots more productive work can be done virtually instead of spending time and money traveling by air to in-person meetings. Anna became excited about the opportunity to modify ways that her firm normally operates and help attract and retain young lawyers.

But Anna knew that changing her law firm's system wouldn't be easy. As a relatively new lawyer who was not a partner, she would need to find allies and use some kind of framework for systems leadership to have the best shot at making measurable progress. If her firm already had a green team of some sort, she could get started with the CLEAR steps within that existing forum. But since there wasn't one, she pointed out to colleagues and supervisors working with her on recruitment that graduating law students are now making law firm choices based on the firm's commitment to sustainability.[4] A new law

Lawyers United for Sustainability (PLUS), Pa. Bar Ass'n, https://www.pabar.org/site/For-Lawyers/Sections/Environmental-and-Energy-Law-Section/Projects-and-Programs/PLUS-Program (last visited May 6, 2022).

2. The Law Firm Sustainability Network offers another set of guidelines, but they are available only to members. Law Firm Sustainability Network, https://lfsnetwork.org/membership/why-join/ (last visited Apr. 12, 2022).

3. Jeff Overton, *Fact Sheet: The Growth in Greenhouse Gas Emissions from Commercial Aviation* (Oct. 17, 2019), Env't & Energy Study Inst., https://www.eesi.org/papers/view/fact-sheet-the-growth-in-greenhouse-gas-emissions-from-commercial-aviation.

4. Law Firm Sustainability Network, CSR & Sustainability: Current State of the Legal Industry Report 2018, https://lfsnetwork.org/media/1170/lfsn-csr-sustainability-survey-report-2018.pdf.

firm partner on her recruitment team, Bill, agreed with Anna that adopting something like the CLAS Guidelines would be a good starting point.

Tim, their newest colleague on the recruitment team, proposed that they simply ask the firm's office manager to have the firm adopt the CLAS Guidelines and some form of the air travel restrictions. The rest of the team explained that this strategy would invite strong pushback from other partners, the board of directors, clients, vendors, and other stakeholders who would feel surprised by not being a part of the process of changing the law firm's system of operation and could undermine the execution of the new policy. Seeking input from the firm's stakeholders would create an opportunity to create buy-in and anticipate problems in forming and executing effective new policies. Anna and Bill agreed to propose convening interested colleagues to discuss possible next steps and invited Tim and others in the firm to participate.

1. Workplace: Convene and Commit

Anna and Bill first brought together a group of interested lawyers in the firm, including many junior attorneys. They then made a commitment to work for a plan that would more fully implement something like the CLAS Guidelines and a new air travel policy.

After reviewing the CLAS Guidelines in more detail, Anna and Bill concluded that most of the 15 recommendations are common sense and that the firm was already doing some of them. For example, Anna and Bill knew that the firm already had a general policy for reducing paper use. They first decided to meet with the firm's office manager, who had been involved in this and some of the other policies covered by the guidelines. The CLAS Guidelines provide a long ready-made list of specific paper-reducing activities the firm could adopt. Using the paper reduction example, Anna and Bill advertised and then hosted a meeting for those in the firm interested in helping the firm become more sustainable. They specifically invited the office manager, knowing that she would play a key role in implementing any policy the firm adopted.

During the meeting they also made the case to their colleagues that the firm ought to adopt a version of the CLAS Guidelines that included a new air travel policy. They explained that adoption of these policies would simply extend the firm's present efforts. They added that no one in this ad hoc group needed to be an expert on sustainability to start working toward this goal. At this first meeting, Anna and Bill asked their eight colleagues who showed up to help assess where the firm was on each of the proposed guidelines. With the office manager's approval, they proposed that after a basic assessment of each guideline, they would approach their superiors and propose that the firm adopt the air travel policy and as many of the guidelines as possible. After a brief discussion, five colleagues agreed to join Anna and Bill in the effort. The team also agreed to a six-month timeline to finish the assessments.

2. Workplace: Look and Learn

Before the next meeting, Anna and Bill mapped their law firm's use of paper to discover patterns of behavior. This approach helped build a shared understanding that the firm's use of paper is excessive and expensive, notwithstanding the paper reduction policy. Other members of the team assessed the firm's use of energy, travel, and other resources relevant to each of the proposed guidelines. They then agreed to make presentations to key leaders in the firm to seek input on what they had learned and gain a better understanding of the best path toward firmwide adoption.

3. Workplace: Engage and Energize

Because continuous engagement among and between participants is so important to successful systems leadership, Anna took advantage of a short conversation she had with Maggie, one of the firm's senior partners, to build momentum. Maggie was delighted to hear about the committee's progress. Anna invited Maggie to the committee's next meeting to get Maggie to emphasize to the group the importance of their work.

While frequent meetings were needed initially, Anna, Bill, and the other committee members decided to limit their continuing in-person meetings to just once a month. To keep the team motivated between meetings, Anna and Bill sent the group a weekly email on progress and convened a happy hour to celebrate progress and build momentum.

4. Workplace: Act with Accountability

Because accountability toward implementing shared goals and principles is so important in any systems leadership effort, Anna and Bill's weekly communication included a report on what each team member learned in their respective guideline area over the past week. A shared drive with a spreadsheet was used to track the week-to-week progress in each guideline area.

At each stage they checked in with the office manager to ensure she was kept abreast of their progress.

After months of work, Jasmine, another committee member, proposed that they not only ask the firm's governing board to adopt sustainability guidelines but also adopt an implementation strategy for the guidelines. Otherwise, Jasmine argued, the guidelines could be meaningless. She explained that the paper reduction policy was not working because it lacked an implementation strategy. The committee liked the idea and drafted a proposal that adoption of the guidelines be accompanied with this implementation strategy:

- Assign a person within the law firm to implement each of the new guidelines by a date certain.
- Establish targets and measures that could be used to track progress.

- Educate all members of the firm about the new guidelines by a date certain.
- Review the guidelines and evaluate their implementation annually, discuss outcomes from the previous year, and make needed changes for the coming year.

5. Workplace: Review and Revise

The committee built a learning-centered process that allowed for engagement by an expanding set of participants. It reviewed its progress regularly and adapted in response to new information or developments. The committee needed to adapt when Ronald, one of the firm's partners, sent a memo to other partners saying that it "seemed" to him that two of the committee members—associates who worked for him—were being distracted from their legal work by their committee participation. Anna, Bill, and the committee went to Maggie, the supportive senior partner at the firm, for advice. Based on Maggie's counsel, Maggie, Anna, and Bill met with Ronald to allay some of his concerns and make adjustments that kept the two associates on the committee without interfering with their work for Ronald.

Maggie also helped the committee arrange a meeting with the office manager and key partners to review the proposed guidelines for possible adoption. At this meeting, Anna and Bill made a compelling case for guideline adoption using information the committee had developed on likely gains in monetary savings and productivity. In this meeting, they demonstrated the high level of commitment that the committee had brought to these issues. Maggie and the other partners praised their leadership, encouraged the office manager to work directly with the committee for six months to finalize the guidelines, and flagged issues that they felt the committee had not yet fully addressed.

The committee continued to meet to respond to these issues and perfect the proposed guidelines. The firm then adopted its first ever sustainability guidelines along with an implementation strategy.

Months later, the office manager was delighted with the cost savings that the sustainability guidelines produced. When Anna came up for a partnership review, her managing partner cited Anna's leadership on this initiative as one key reason for her elevation to partner.

When the sustainability guidelines were put on the firm website and inserted into the firm's advertisements for associate recruiting, several new hires cited the guidelines as a contributing factor in their decisions to join the firm.

In sum, the story of Anna, Bill, and their ad hoc team illustrates one way that lawyers new to sustainability can apply systems leadership to implement sustainable development principles in the workplace.

9

Sustainable Development Lawyers as Systems Leaders in Communities

The previous two chapters discussed systems leadership for sustainable development in law practice and in the law office. Systems leadership also positions lawyers to effect larger changes, including changes in the community. This chapter again uses a hypothetical story to show how the CLEAR process for systems leadership described in Chapter 7 can play out in this context.

Pat is a lawyer at a nonprofit organization that helps veterans train for and secure good-paying clean energy jobs. Pat was the first from her family to graduate from college, and she took on an enormous amount of debt to pay for law school. Her first job was at the state's natural resources agency, where she distinguished herself.

Pat leased an electric vehicle (EV) a year earlier and was convinced that EV charging stations would eventually be ubiquitous, so she thought that accelerating the pace of EV charging station installations in her community might be a good way for her to make a difference. For Pat, this was also personal. The owner of the apartment complex where she lived had talked about installing an EV charging station in the complex's parking lot but had decided against it. He argued that it was more important to keep rents low than to install EV charging stations and pass the costs on to the tenants.

The city council had previously discussed incentives to put more charging stations throughout the city, including in the part of town where Pat lived. But because wealthier people in the city with EVs had the money to set up EV charging at their own homes, making EV charging stations available for lower-income residents and throughout the community never gained momentum. A year later, not much had changed; Pat still had to drive across town to charge her EV.

One night when she got home, she asked the apartment owner again about the possibility of installing an apartment complex EV charging station. Predictably, he said no. But this time, Pat decided to do something. She put a message on the apartment complex bulletin board asking other tenants to call her if they wanted to talk about addressing the issue.

The next day, she got a call from Ahmed, who lived in the same complex. Ahmed also had an EV and shared her frustration and agreed to join her effort to get EV charging at the apartment complex. Impressed by her legal skills and organizational thinking, he suggested that Pat lead an effort to petition the city council to adopt an ordinance installing EV stations and incentivizing private entities to do the same.

After talking with Ahmed and a few other neighbors who supported their EV charging station ideas, she saw that few of them had the skills that would be necessary to bring people together, develop shared goals, and create a structure and then a strategy to produce more EV charging stations. Working with a diverse set of laypeople in her community would be different than organizing lawyers at work. To help Ahmed understand her thinking and gain leadership skills, Pat shared with him the CLEAR process for systems leadership.

1. Community: Convene and Commit

With the help of Ahmed and Roy, a car dealer across town who was interested in selling more EVs, Pat moderated a dialogue with interested tenants to address the issue. Pat's initial goal was to get tenants to pressure the apartment owner to install one or more EV charging stations. She learned at the meeting that city, state, and federal incentives would matter greatly in getting charging stations installed at the apartment complex and throughout the city.

Pat and Ahmed studied the CLEAR guidelines and concluded that they needed more help. They researched and discussed who in their city and state were key stakeholders for getting EV charging stations approved and built. Fortunately, because of Pat's legal connections with other environmental lawyers, she was able to quickly find Simon, the policy director at one of the state's foremost nonprofit organizations, who was focused on EV infrastructure. Through Simon, Pat and her community quickly gained valuable information about local, state, and national stakeholders who could provide more information and support.

Simon introduced Pat to Robin, a community organizer in Pat's city who expressed interest in joining the effort. Pat and Ahmed invited Robin and a growing list of residents to a meeting at the apartment complex to talk about the effort. As the meeting date approached, Pat learned that Robin had successfully organized numerous campaigns in her own city on behalf of low-income residents. Pat and Ahmed quickly arranged a premeeting with Robin to explain their aim to use the CLEAR framework for systems leadership as their guide. Robin had never heard the term "systems leadership," nor did she know about the CLEAR framework. But after reviewing the elements of the CLEAR framework, she explained that each step in it pretty much described what she had done as a community organizer for many years. Robin agreed to help them organize the upcoming meeting and develop next steps for the group to at least get EV charging stations in the apartment complex, if not in the rest of the city.

During the meeting, they made the case for installing at least two EV charging stations in the apartment complex parking lot. Robin explained that no one in this group needed to be an expert on EVs or sustainability to start working toward this goal. Of the twelve people who showed up to the meeting, seven committed to work with them to help build the proposal and present it to the apartment owner. These seven people also agreed to advocate for an EV ordinance to the city council.

At the meeting, some in the group talked about first going to the city council to see if it would provide the apartment complex some kind of incentive for EV charging installation. Several in attendance argued that any eventual "ask" of the council might be stronger if they could demonstrate they had already tried to persuade the apartment complex owner to install the chargers. After a robust discussion, they decided to move first with the apartment owner while planning to address the city council later.

2. Community: Look and Learn

To inform themselves on the issues, one subgroup agreed to collect existing information on past efforts to get apartment complexes to install EV charging stations. Another subgroup agreed to start looking at possible city policies to incentivize EV charging station installation.

As a result of several meetings, the neighbors built a shared understanding of the components, actors, dynamics, and influences that were barriers to the installation of an adequate EV charging infrastructure, generating new insights and ideas. As they built trust among themselves, others shared their experiences in trying to motivate change with other apartment managers and the city council. With Robin's help, Pat took on the role of educating the group on their collective learning, guiding new efforts, and integrating the neighbors into a coherent team. After one of their meetings they devised a dual strategy focused on both public and private systems of governance. First, they would work to get private apartment complexes like theirs to install EV charging stations. Second, they would work to persuade public entities like the city council to purchase some EVs for the city's fleet of cars, install charging stations throughout the city (including in low-income neighborhoods), and institute incentives for private entities to do the same.

Pat realized that if the group were to have any chance at persuading the city council to adopt new policies to enable more EV charging stations throughout the city, her group was going to need to educate the council and its staff about the best laws that local governments are already adopting for EVs. Fortunately, Pat had learned about a shortcut to finding a strong EV policy to offer the city, a new legal tool with a collection of updated local, state, and federal greenhouse-gas-reducing policies, Model Laws for Deep Decarbonization in the United States, www.lpdd.org.[1] Instead of having to draft a new EV

1. *Model Laws for Deep Decarbonization in the United States*, Columbia Law Sch. Sabin Ctr. for Climate Change & Widener Univ. Commw. Law Sch.

ordinance, the city could consider adopting similar ordinances already enacted elsewhere and model ordinances drafted by experts.

3. Community: Engage and Energize

Since Ahmed held a job as a writer of online sales advertisements, Pat volunteered to collect the email addresses of those in their group so each could receive a monthly email from Ahmed about the group's progress and next steps. This activity and others built trust, commitment, and collaboration among the neighbors. Inspiration, incentives, and milestones helped to drive progress and maintain momentum. Each month they organized a potluck dinner at the apartment complex. At each dinner, Roy brought different EVs to attract participation and let group members enjoy inspecting the newest EV models and hear about what models might be coming down the pike.

4. Community: Act with Accountability

As with any system change effort, establishing and maintaining accountability for the many varied efforts under way to achieve the dual initiatives at the apartment complex and at the city council became crucial to success. That is where Robin's community organizing experience came to bear. Robin was able to mirror some of her past work to build an easy-to-use tracking system for key efforts underway and the people responsible for advancing them.

At one point, they convinced a city council member to meet with their apartment owner to brainstorm what kind of incentives he would need to install EV charging stations. Prepared with the www.lpdd.org tool the group provided him, the city council member promised the group that he would bring the tool and the issue to the council staff for an assessment and a report at a future public meeting.

As more meetings occurred and the initiative matured, Pat's skills as a lawyer enabled her to build coordination and governance structures that accelerated the group's momentum. That is, she was

---

Env't Law & Sustainability Ctr., https://lpdd.org/ (last visited Apr. 11, 2022). *See also* Sustainable Dev. Code, https://sustainablecitycode.org/ (last visited Apr. 12, 2022).

organized, held regular meetings and kept minutes, listened carefully to the needs and concerns of the volunteers, anticipated problems, and worked with others to resolve them quickly.

That momentum included a meeting with the apartment complex owner. Before the meeting, Roy, the EV seller, suggested that the team propose to the apartment owner an exchange of sorts. He suggested that in exchange for the apartment owner installing two EV charging stations at the complex, they could help solve a different problem the apartment owner had—full occupancy. Because the apartment complex was never fully occupied with tenants, Roy proposed that he and the group advertise the complex in a wide range of online and social media networks as a great place to live. This would be free advertising for the apartment owner. The group agreed to hone the idea, after which they presented it at the meeting with the apartment owner. To the group's surprise, the owner agreed to the concept in principle but then said that his "lawyer might have issues." To overcome the hurdle and maintain momentum, Pat said that she, as a lawyer, would be happy to meet with the complex owner's lawyer to overcome any potential legal issues. When the local housing market strengthened several months later and the occupancy problem disappeared, the apartment owner lost interest in this advertising exchange. Nonetheless, the apartment owner gained a new respect for the group, a respect that would be an important factor in later efforts. At the same time, the group kept pressure on the city council to buy EVs, build public charging stations, and create incentives for private installation of EV chargers.

5. Community: Review and Revise

The group reviewed progress regularly and modified their initiative and strategy accordingly. Progress was slow on a citywide solution. Pat's group continued to build relationships as they worked on this issue, considered other approaches, and identified people who could help. Eventually, the city council member introduced the apartment owner to an investor to explore the possibility of setting up a pilot project. The investor would pay the cost of installing EV stations in a city parking lot adjacent to the apartment complex in exchange for low-cost EV charging user fees. The investor said this location would provide more people with access to the charging stations, including lower-income people. Everyone agreed. With the city's consent, the investor had two charging stations installed within six months.

The group planned a party to celebrate their success. But by now, with a growing group of people in the area who wanted more EV charging stations, they resolved to keep going to create an EV charging system throughout the city. To help make that happen, they persuaded the local TV station to come to the party and do a story about the organizing effort. Ahmed's subsequent communications drew increasingly helpful media attention and new volunteers. The growing group then began meeting with not only the city council and staff but also state and federal elected officials to ensure that public governance efforts to create more EV charging stations were coordinated in a mutually beneficial fashion. On the private governance side, the group began building relationships with leaders at the state apartment owners' association to garner support for public governance incentives that apartment owners might actually utilize to install more EV charging stations.

News about the group's efforts also reached advocates for low-income persons, who argued that the city should focus on broadening access to public transportation, particularly buses, and encourage alternatives to driving. Robin, the community organizer, advised Pat to meet with these advocates and find a way to join forces with them. After several meetings, the apartment group revised its agenda in response to these advocates, a move that brought new allies and political support.

Many in Pat's apartment group were energized as they saw things slowly move forward, and each small step in the right direction produced additional motivation. A year later, in large part because of the group and its new allies, the city council adopted a suite of EV charging ordinances, including incentives for apartment owners and others to install EV stations and a program for installing charging stations citywide. The city council also expanded bus service in low-income neighborhoods and began a process to revise its zoning and transportation requirements to make the city more walkable.

As she made a difference, Pat developed an invaluable set of leadership skills that she then applied in other contexts, including in her law practice. Her systems leadership work for sustainable development distinguished her and earned her public gratitude and professional advancement.

This story shows some of the ways that systems leadership by lawyers can work for sustainable development in communities. Figure 9.1 emphasizes the importance of integrating leadership with key points from previous chapters. While we hope this story is informative, the basic lessons of lawyers using systems leadership are best learned by practice.

Figure 9.1 Difference Maker—Version 5

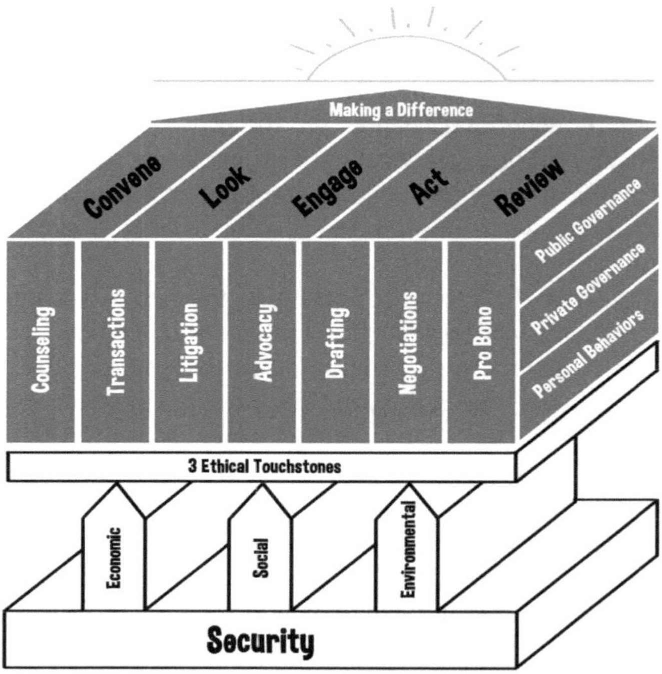

10

The Rewards and Frustrations of Sustainable Development Work in Law Practice

In previous chapters, we have discussed how to get started on sustainability leadership (Chapter 5), how to use the sustainable development framework to advise clients (Chapter 6), and how to exercise leadership for sustainable development in a variety of contexts (Chapters 7, 8, and 9). This chapter focuses on your likely personal experience in doing this work. Understanding the most rewarding and frustrating aspects of sustainable development work in the law can prepare you to thrive as your leadership journey evolves. To be sure, any legal work has rewarding and frustrating aspects. But the rewards and frustrations described here are particularly common in sustainability work. This chapter, like some earlier chapters, reflects the collected views of experienced sustainability law practitioners.

1. Sustainable Development Legal Work Has Many Rewarding Aspects

a. Making a Positive Difference

Many lawyers describe the most rewarding aspect of their work in terms of specific projects or laws to which they contributed, where they made positive differences that they can see. Another lawyer says the work is "always about the good I'm doing." A lawyer who specializes in sustainable community development projects says:

> The thing I find most rewarding is when we get to create a project that truly makes the community better than it would have been without the project. This is a really high standard. So much development diminishes the community. It is so hard to deliver development that not just sustains but makes things better. That is the standard I strive for when working for sustainable development.

Another attorney explains the potential for sustainable development to accomplish good outside of the United States, particularly in developing countries where many of this attorney's clients operate:

> On a global geopolitical level, it is the opportunity to create extraordinary good in places that should not have to experience primitive and benighted approaches or walk the same resource-intensive pathways to prosperity for their people as developed countries did. There are generation-skipping technologies and theories. If an advanced solid waste sorting technology could be implemented in Nairobi, for example, you could remanufacture or up-manufacture up to 95 percent of what is currently being disposed of.

Many attribute the ability to do this kind of work to their clients. "You collect enough clients that want to do the right thing," says an energy finance lawyer, "then you get to do the right thing most of the time." This lawyer added that it is "getting better all the time."

While many find satisfaction in getting specific projects done, others express satisfaction in drafting laws that are subsequently enacted or in helping to get ordinances or laws adopted. One attorney, who helped write the regulations for a five-cent tax for plastic bags for a major city, said that "seeing this in operation is amazing."

Another—whose work in drafting and implementing laws at the state level has led to significant reductions in that state's greenhouse gas emissions—has found such "structural reform" especially satisfying.

Some are nonetheless bluntly cautious or circumspect about the limits of what they are helping to achieve. Many cast their work in terms of reducing negative impacts rather than in terms of achieving positive impacts. One lawyer makes a difference "on some days." That said, the opportunities to make a difference are rewarding.

b. Persuading Clients to Move in a More Sustainable Direction

Others find satisfaction in explaining to clients why more sustainable approaches are better and how they will work. One enjoys "persuading companies to invest in a new technology that is truly better, safer, and more efficacious than something that has been used for years." Another, who specializes in legal work related to sustainable communities, says, "The part I love the best is rolling out that master plan with the client and spending hours talking about the possible things that could happen with this property."

Many find particular satisfaction in convincing skeptical clients. This explanation is illustrative: "I love it when people who are so certain that what they want to do is right for the world realize that a lower-cost, less intrusive solution is in fact better for the environment."

c. Intellectual Engagement

Some attorneys emphasize that they find the work enjoyable and intellectually engaging. "It is fun," one attorney says. Another describes it as "an endless horizon. That's the most exciting thing. It is just beginning, and you can't see where it will go." Another, with a long and diverse career in the public and private sector, says:

> What is wonderful about this field is that it is so diverse. It never ceases to engage me intellectually. My career has been very multidimensional—it has been sustaining and nurturing. I can't think of another career that has been as sustaining and challenging. By contrast, I know a lawyer who has been a bankruptcy lawyer for 35 years, and this has been a very static area of law. Sustainability is a very dynamic area of law, policy, and thought leadership.

d. Opportunity to Work with Great People

Some express their greatest satisfaction in terms of the talented and diverse people with whom they get to work. One explains this as "having a community of people in your office [whom you] can work with to realize the vision of sustainability." Another says: "People who work in sustainability tend to be very nice. This is not a joke; it is true. They are interested in cooperation, working across department lines, and encouraging departments to look at alternatives and options to be more sustainable."

While sustainable development legal work can be rewarding, sometimes it is not. Your experiences might produce a wide range of expressions, even on the same day, like those shown in the illustration below.

2. Sustainable Development Legal Work Also Has Frustrating or Less Enjoyable Aspects

Many lawyers say they find little or nothing unpleasant or frustrating about their sustainability work. Others describe a range of aspects of this work that they find frustrating or do not enjoy.

a. Narrow-Minded Clients

Many complain about some of their clients, often distinguishing between clients with whom they enjoy working and clients with whom they do not: "I meet clients who want to be best in the field and clients who are dragged into the field kicking and screaming," one attorney explains. A common complaint from these lawyers is about clients engaged in "narrow, short-term thinking." One attorney describes such clients as "focused purely on minimizing short-term cost—how much you pay to settle the case or close the deal, and how much you pay your lawyer to do it." Another common complaint is clients who lack a basic "understanding of science and policy behind sustainability and environmental protection" (e.g., climate change, chemical loading) or who resist attorney suggestions "based not on facts but on politics." The attorneys say that these and other factors often mean that those clients are not interested in analyzing a problem from a sustainability perspective or looking at the additional options that a sustainability analysis would provide.

An attorney who has done a lot of work on cleaning up contaminated sites explains these problems in terms of the "limited role of the attorney in big picture decision-making." This attorney said:

> When I talk to clients about what they are going to do next, after the property is cleaned up, [about whether they are] going to do a green building, etc., that falls on deaf ears. There is a perception that energy efficiency and green building are more expensive than they really are. My overall frustration is not getting a place at the table in the overall conversation.

b. Public Opposition

Another group of lawyers says that the most frustrating aspect of their sustainability work is public opposition, based on ideology or outright misrepresentation, to specific proposals or projects. A lawyer who does considerable legal work for solar industry clients complains about the "blowback that the industry gets from people who are not knowledgeable." In one case, this lawyer's client proposed a solar energy project for a school system that had demonstrable economic advantages, but one school board member was simply opposed to solar energy. Another echoes that point in describing the least enjoyable aspect of sustainability work:

> Ideological intransigence; that's number one, head and shoulders above everything else. It is a whole cluster of things. If I have an American value, it is that we recognize problems soberly and solve them intelligently. When people talk about socialism, conspiracy, property rights—this requires an entirely different skill set, and it impedes problem-solving.

One complains about the "Not in My Back Yard" (NIMBY) phenomenon that occurs on some of the land use projects on which this attorney works:

> The most frustrating thing is when individuals or communities use legitimate sustainability issues to mask raw NIMBYism. Say a community really [does not] want adjoining development to happen. So they raise issues about trees or endangered species that they have not cared about historically; they simply don't want development on the adjoining property. We can't work out a compromise on that issue because they are using it as a blocking issue. This gives a bad name to legitimate issues, because developers and engineers then see these simply as things to stop the project.

c. Lack of Public Understanding

Another group of lawyers says that what they like least is not public opposition but rather the lack of public understanding. For some, this is based on the same concerns—about the lack of basic science and environmental-policy knowledge—as they often have about their clients. For others, there is a distinct regional dimension to this ignorance. One attorney who frequently travels to California says sustainability "is in the dark ages in my home state." In this attorney's view, that ignorance translates into having fewer clients available for sustainability-related legal work. Another attorney does not enjoy the "need to win the same battles over and over again." This attorney explains: "You can go to the state legislature and argue that energy efficiency would save money and reduce emissions. Then five years later you have to go back and defend the same program because it is threatened with budget cuts."

d. Legal Barriers to Sustainability and Difficult Approval Processes

Some lawyers identify legal barriers, and the time and difficulty of getting sustainability projects and actions done, as the part of their work that they like least. Within this group, a common complaint is that the laws themselves get in the way. One criticized a township code that requires LEED projects to get a variance for energy-efficient lighting and waterless urinals, rather than simply allowing them. The variance requirement adds time and expense to these projects because of the need to prove that a variance is warranted. A land use lawyer frequently butts against "wrongheaded legislation that won't let us do the best possible plan," such as requirements for more parking spaces than are needed for a particular place.

For others, the difficulty of navigating existing laws and policies to get more sustainable projects and activities approved is what they like least. One complains how difficult it is to satisfy all stakeholders for a proposed project or activity, saying that "99 percent of the time not everyone is going to be happy." Another complains how bureaucracy and lengthy review processes for complex projects (in a municipal setting) can "wear you down." This lawyer says it can also wear clients down. Hopefully, the lawyer adds, they "stay the course and stay enthusiastic."

These are some of the personal rewards and frustrations in doing sustainability law work. Over time we expect the increasing numbers of lawyers who do this work will increase the rewards and reduce the frustrations.

11

The Future of Sustainable Development in Law Practice

Sustainable development in law practice will grow because clients will demand it and because lawyers bring important skills to the table for making it happen. As we stated in the introduction, sustainable development may be one of the most important ideas to come out of the 20th century. As the idea of sustainable development continues to take hold, it will be of increasing importance in law practice. But it will not happen automatically. The key to integrating sustainable development in the practice of law as soon as possible rests with lawyers—including you.

1. Clients Will Increasingly Demand Legal Assistance to Address Sustainable Development

The compounding enormity of the world's economic, social, environmental, and security challenges—outlined in Chapters 1 and 2—is creating great pressure for the legal system to respond. The 2015 Final Report of the Sustainable Development Task Force of the American Bar Association states:

> Going forward, lawyers will need to become involved in a broad range of sustainability issues. Younger lawyers, who represent the future of the legal profession, often understand these issues better than the lawyers who would hire them. The transition to sustainability in both governmental and private sector decision-making is inevitable and will profoundly affect the legal profession.[1]

Though the pace of progress has been woefully inadequate, pressures for sustainable development will increase and almost certainly prompt the adoption of new and modified laws at all levels of government. That, in turn, will require an enormous amount of additional and thoughtful work by lawyers. The growth and development of private law for sustainability also requires considerable legal work. As corporations seek to reduce their greenhouse gas emissions, for example, there is a growing need for private law (Environmental, Social, and Governance; supply chain agreements; and the like) to ensure that these pollution reductions are effectuated.

In addition, a growing number of clients will seek advice, not just on compliance with existing laws or in anticipation of future laws, but on how to chart a legally durable course for a sustainable future. In fact, a growing number of corporate clients, seeking to make their supply chain more sustainable, see lawyers as part of their supply chain. They send questionnaires to law firms on their approach to sustainability before engaging their services. Because virtually every field of law involves sustainable development in specific and significant ways, practitioners in all fields need to be knowledgeable about sustainable development and incorporate it into their practice. This reality greatly enlarges the number and type of lawyers who need to be—and will be—involved in this work.

The social dimension of sustainability also expands the number of needed lawyers. A corporate social responsibility lawyer explains:

> The expansion of social equity within sustainability has resulted in new types of positions. If you put social equity in sustainability, there is an expansion of roles for lawyers. Most of the expansion I've seen in sustainability positions has been inside corporations. Since 2008, there are a lot more

1. Am. Bar Ass'n Task Force on Sustainable Dev., Final Report 4 (2015).

sustainability positions that lawyers can fill that exist in large-scale corporations.

A lawyer with experience in sustainable development in corporate law says there will be many more sustainability law jobs in the future:

> As the world changes to embrace sustainability principles, the legal jobs will change everywhere. It will be infused in so many elements of corporate behavior that it will become a language you need to be familiar with, to speak, to do the job you are doing, just as you need to understand math to do the things you do. That flavor will be in every legal job. That will be the evolution of sustainability-related entities and objectives, percolating into societal behavior, corporate behavior, and interpersonal behavior.

Sustainable development will also be used more in law practice because it builds on a growing sustainable development movement in the United States and elsewhere,[2] a movement in which clients will need to participate. In doing so, clients will need not only legal work but also thoughtful leadership from lawyers. This movement is reflected in the sustainable development work of colleges and universities, communities, governments, and corporations; it is reflected in the development and use of renewable energy, energy-efficient technologies, green buildings, green infrastructure, green products, and safer and better chemicals and medicines; greater employee rights; and increased diversity, equity, and inclusion, to name a few key subject-matter areas. This movement is reflected in the work done by organizations in every sector, in for-profit, nonprofit, for-benefit, and governmental organizations, and at every level of society—in local communities, in states, and nationally as well as in our international systems of trade and governance. This movement also responds to the tragic violations of human rights, national sovereignty, and other international laws by authoritarian regimes (e.g., the Russian invasion of Ukraine)—which are deeply antagonistic to sustainable development. All of these require legal work and leadership.

As noted in Chapter 5, the ABA House of Delegates has emphasized three times the role that lawyers need to play in realizing a

2. John C. Dernbach et al., Acting as If Tomorrow Matters: Accelerating the Transition to Sustainability 285–300 (2012).

sustainable society, most recently in 2013. The report accompanying the 2013 resolution called on lawyers, law firms, and other law organizations to "[e]ncourage and support sustainability efforts by their clients, and raise sustainability issues with clients at appropriate times," giving clients "useful advice not only on legal compliance but also on options that sustainability and sustainability tools can provide for them."[3]

Even with the narrower challenge of addressing climate change, and the critiques of the legal profession as being far too slow in enlisting its members to lead in combating it, there are some promising signs of progress. The 2019 American Bar Association House of Delegates resolution, which we mentioned in Chapter 4, urges lawyers "to advise their clients of the risks and opportunities that climate change provides."[4]

Similarly, the 2020 International Bar Association (IBA) Climate Crisis Statement, also mentioned in Chapter 4, "urges lawyers, acting in accordance with their professional conduct rules and the rule of law, to consider . . . taking a climate conscious approach to problems encountered in daily legal practice." This includes "advising clients of the potential risks, liability, and reputational damage arising from activity that negatively contributes to the climate crisis." The IBA statement also "urges lawyers, as influential figures and thought leaders within society, to live responsibly in the face of the climate crisis" by reducing "their environmental footprint" in "everyday actions" and by "supporting positive changes in the workplace, including adoption of more sustainable practices, such as greater reliance on electronic file storage facilities and digital technologies, more energy efficient offices, and more climate-friendly travel and procurement choices."[5]

Importantly, the report accompanying the 2013 ABA sustainable development resolution, as well as the 2019 ABA climate change resolution and the 2020 IBA statement, all support changes in law. The report accompanying the ABA sustainable development resolution

3. Am. Bar Ass'n House of Delegates, Res. 105, at 8, 9 (2013), https://www.americanbar.org/content/dam/aba/administrative/office_president/2013_hod_annual_meeting_105.authcheckdam.pdf.

4. Am. Bar Ass'n House of Delegates, Res. 111 (2019), https://www.americanbar.org/content/dam/aba/directories/policy/annual-2019/111-annual-2019.pdf.

5. Int'l Bar Ass'n, Climate Crisis Statement (2020), https://www.ibanet.org/MediaHandler?id=822c1967-f851-4819-8200-2fe298164922.

said "federal, state, local, territorial and tribal governments should adopt or modify legislation, regulations and policies, to effectuate the transition to sustainability."[6] The ABA climate resolution urges all levels of government as well as the private sector "to recognize their obligation to address climate change and take action" to "reduce U.S. greenhouse gas emissions to net zero or below as soon as possible, consistent with the latest peer-reviewed science."[7] The IBA statement "encourages lawyers to engage with current and future legislative and policymaking efforts to address the climate crisis."[8]

Likewise, many of the mainstream businesses that attorneys represent appear to be recognizing these realities and urging a better response on issues critical to sustainable development. For example, in 2019 the Business Roundtable formally recognized that the purpose of corporations includes "embracing sustainable practices across our businesses" and that customers, employees, suppliers, and communities are to be considered essential stakeholders.[9] In 2020, it issued a statement urging deep cuts in U.S. greenhouse gas emissions.[10] All of this suggests that professional and business norms are moving toward recognition that lawyers have a responsibility to work for sustainable development and to overcome one of its key barriers, climate disruption. Many individual corporations, but not all, recognize this evolving climate action norm.

This growing momentum on climate action comes from other sources as well. Market forces are driving down the costs of clean energy and increasing the need for legal help with clean energy projects. Investors are increasing pressure on corporations to disclose the accelerating risks of climate change, and the public is demanding less-harmful consumer products. Law students and young lawyers, who want to make a contribution and to work in law offices or other organizations that value their views and aspirations, are an especially important force for recognition of an attorney's responsibility.

---

6. Res. 105, *supra* note 3, at 9.

7. Res. 111, *supra* note 4.

8. Climate Crisis Statement, *supra* note 5.

9. *Statement on the Purpose of a Corporation*, BUS. ROUNDTABLE (2019), https://s3.amazonaws.com/brt.org/BRT-StatementonthePurposeofaCorporationJuly2021.pdf.

10. BUS. ROUNDTABLE, ADDRESSING CLIMATE CHANGE: PRINCIPLES AND POLICIES (2020), https://s3.amazonaws.com/brt.org/Business-RoundtableAddressingClimateChangeReport.September2020.pdf.

This growing movement for sustainable development is girded by three basic realities. First, sustainable development leads to a higher quality of life for all people. By achieving multiple benefits (social, economic, environmental, security) at the same time, sustainable development can deliver more benefits than conventional development can produce and, as a result of the integrated decision-making process, with far fewer costs (social, economic, environmental, security). Indeed, in fields where sustainable development has made the most progress, like those identified earlier, it has done so because it is plainly more attractive than conventional development.[11]

Second, sustainable development is economically attractive. As we look ahead to a more crowded world with increased economic activity and growing social, environmental, and security threats, the only economic activity that will be durable, profitable, and job creating is that which is sustainable. This is not feel-good optimism; it simply reflects the reality in which we live. Just as "business as usual" will not work, "law as usual" will not work either. Without changes in law and lawyering, the needed changes will come too slowly and unevenly to avoid the worst effects of unsustainable development, including climate change.

Third, advancing sustainable development is the right thing for lawyers to do.[12] As leadership expert Michael Fullan has written, "You cannot move substantially toward sustainability in the absence of a widely shared moral purpose."[13] A key factual premise of sustainable development is that weak economies, environmental damage, systemic racism, and wars of aggression all hurt other humans, including humans who are not yet born. Unsustainable development, in other words, is unjust for both the present and future generations. As we noted earlier, this sensitivity to the needs of future generations is embedded in American law. As the preamble to the U.S. Constitution makes clear, its authors intended its benefits to extend "to ourselves and our posterity."[14] When people come to understand what unsustainable development means, they often begin to see sustainable

11. DERNBACH ET AL., *supra* note 2, at 285, 289.

12. *Id.* at 290.

13. MICHAEL FULLAN, LEADERSHIP & SUSTAINABILITY: SYSTEMS THINKERS IN ACTION 87 (2005).

14. U.S. CONST. pmbl.

alternatives as aligned with their beliefs, attitudes, and moral compass, as expressions of who they are and what they want.

Principles such as intergenerational equity that are at the core of sustainable development can have dramatic emotional and intellectual power when taken seriously. Pope Francis I explains intergenerational equity in a way that resonates within the Catholic religion as well as other faiths and philosophical traditions. "Once we start to think about the kind of world we are leaving to future generations, we look at things differently," the pontiff says. "We realize that the world is a gift which we have freely received and must share with others. Since the world has been given to us, we can no longer view reality in a purely utilitarian way, in which efficiency and productivity are entirely geared to our individual benefit."[15]

Other widely held values include the injunction to do no harm. Professor Victor Flatt, who teaches at the University of Houston Law Center, explains that "the individual has a right to be free from any externally imposed harm."[16] Additional powerful norms that support sustainable development include national security, conservation, prudent stewardship, accountability for the consequences of one's actions, and the precautionary approach. Ultimately, clients and the people who work for them tend to care deeply about at least some of these principles.

All of this means that clients will increasingly demand that their attorneys have the knowledge and skills to work for sustainable development.

2. More Lawyers Will Use Their Skills to Help Achieve a Sustainable Society

Law, as we have discussed, will play an essential role in the transition to a more sustainable society. And lawyers have unique access to common levers of societal change—how the law is applied and how the law is reformed. As we discussed in Chapter 3, lawyers have a moral responsibility to work for a more sustainable society. This book has provided evidence of the many ways in which lawyers are already

15. Pope Francis I, Laudato Si ¶ 159 (2015).

16. Victor B. Flatt, *This Land Is Your Land (Our Right to the Environment)*, 107 W. Va. L. Rev. 1, 27 (2004).

doing this. While these lawyers are, sadly, comparatively few in number at present, we believe more lawyers will respond to the demands described earlier.

Our more basic hope is that lawyers like you will not simply respond to these demands; they will help lead the effort to achieve a more sustainable society. Lawyers should spread the word and organize others in ways appropriate to their circumstances. The challenges of sustainable development, including the need to address climate change, are considerable, and so are the opportunities. But there is a finite and rapidly closing window for effectively addressing these issues. Like all professionals and all people, attorneys have a responsibility to preserve our planet and our quality of life. In our specific professional roles and, more broadly, as lawyers, we have a special responsibility for the quality of justice and the public good. We need to talk about these issues and how to address them and encourage all lawyers to participate. We also need to share legal tools and approaches that work and support each other in doing so. And in a variety of ways, as the third touchstone in Chapter 3 states, we need to advance justice, law reform, and the public interest. Among other things, we must work harder for law reform for sustainable development—for repeal or modification of laws that impede sustainable practices and for enactment and implementation of new local, state, federal, and international laws as well as private governance instruments.

We can urge law schools and bar associations to teach lawyers and law students about sustainable development and systems leadership in the law. Such courses can jumpstart a lawyer's sustainability journey. Lawyers can urge their employers to become educated on these topics and apply these principles, hire and promote those lawyers who excel at this work, and lead any number of initiatives to help themselves, clients, and society using these principles. Lawyers can make presentations to bar associations and community groups about how sustainable development principles can be successfully applied. Moving from individual actions to collective actions is necessary, but it starts with individuals. As cultural anthropologist Margaret Mead was quoted as saying, "Never doubt that a small group of thoughtful, committed people can change the world. Indeed, it is the only thing that ever has."[17]

---

17. Donald Keys, Earth at Omega: Passage to Planetization 79 (1982) (epigraph attributed to Margaret Mead).

Figure 11.1 Difference Maker—Version 6

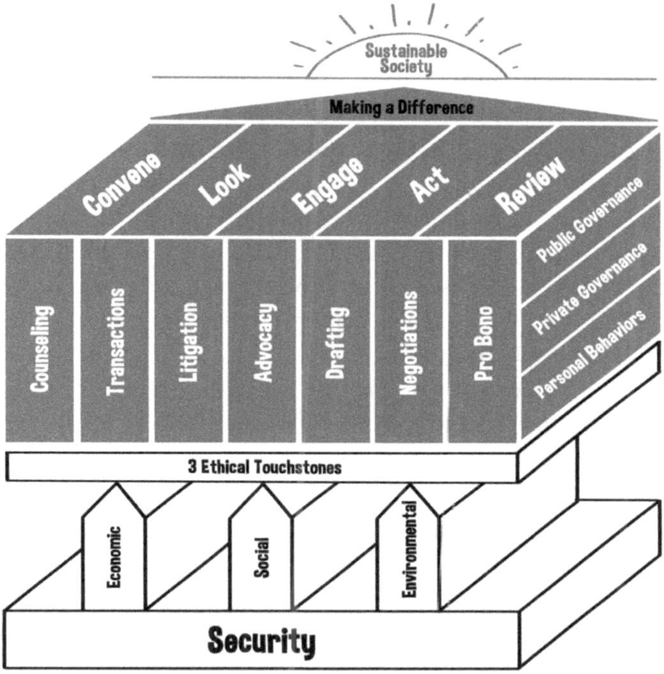

The final version of the Difference Maker illustration, shown in Figure 11.1, summarizes the main points of this guide. It shows the four fundamentals of a sustainable society and how each of us, as a lawyer, is in a unique position to lead society's transition, combining ethics and our legal skills with leadership.

With more lawyers putting this guide and other resources to good use, we can build the momentum we need to transform our work, our profession, and society to achieve far more sustainable outcomes.

In J.R.R. Tolkien's *The Lord of the Rings*, the main character, Frodo, laments his fate of living in trying times. The wizard Gandalf responds, "So do I and so do all who live to see such times. But that is not for them to decide. All we have to decide is what to do with the time that is given us."[18]

18. J.R.R. Tolkien, The Lord of the Rings: Fellowship of the Ring 55–56 (2018).

Similarly, in his 2011 book, *The Great Work*, Thomas Berry described the Great Work that the state of the world has imposed on this generation:

> The success or failure of any historical age is the extent to which those living at that time have fulfilled the special role that history has imposed upon them. No age lives completely unto itself. Each age has only what is received from prior generations. Just now we have abundant evidence that the various species of life, the mountains and rivers, and even the vast ocean itself, which we once thought beyond serious impact from humans, will survive only in their damaged integrity. The Great Work before us, the task of moving modern industrial civilization from its present devastating influence on the Earth to a more benign mode of presence, is not a role that we have chosen. It is a role given to us, beyond any consultation with ourselves. We did not choose. We were chosen by some power beyond ourselves to fulfill this historical task. . . . We are, as it were, thrown into existence with a challenge and a role that is beyond any personal choice. The nobility of our lives, however, depends upon the manner in which we come to understand and fulfill our assigned role.[19]

We hope this guide will help you play a role in this Great Work. The challenges are great, and so are the rewards.

19. Thomas Berry, The Great Work: Our Way into the Future 7 (1999).